Advanced Harmony, Melody & Composition

PAUL STURMAN

Professor of Harmony and Composition
at the London College of Music

LONGMAN

LONGMAN GROUP UK LIMITED
Longman House
Burnt Mill, Harlow, Essex CM20 2JE, England
and Associated Companies throughout the world

First published 1986
Second impression 1988

Set in 10/12pt Times Roman on a Lasercomp system

*Produced by Longman Group (FE) Limited
Printed in Hong Kong*

ISBN 0-582-35441-2

Contents

1 Writing for the piano: harmony 5

Writing for the piano: melody 14

2 Suspensions and pedal points 18

Words and music 31

3 Seventh chords 39

Writing for the piano: accompaniments to songs 48

4 Chromatic harmony: secondary dominants 61

Style in melody writing 71

5 Modulation to the dominant 84

Phrase symmetry and balance 91

6 Modulation to other closely related keys 96

Contrasting phrases 103

7 Modulation from the minor to closely related keys 107

Asymmetrical phrases 115

8 Sequences in harmony 118

Three-phrase form 126

9 Harmony and modulating melodies 130

Four-phrase plans 139

10 The diminished seventh chord 145

Two-part form 153

11 Harmony and the chorale 160

Three-part form 171

12 Ninth chords 180

Melody from harmony 189

13 Borrowed chords and altered chords 196

Melodic and harmonic rhythm 207

14 Modulation to remote keys 219

The use of music and its influence on form 232

Acknowledgements 238

Introduction

Music is a mixture of many ingredients – melody, harmony, rhythm and form. A good composition, whether a Bach fugue or a song by the Beatles, combines these ingredients in a complete and unified way. Many harmony textbooks treat them in isolation, laying out the theory of the subject as a method, and abstract harmony exercises are completed by the student in the hope of gaining a technical knowledge of the subject. Perhaps this is why some find the study of harmony difficult and rather boring. So often it seems to be a thing apart, cut off somehow from the real world of music.

Advanced Harmony, Melody and Composition carries on from where *Harmony, Melody and Composition* finished. The approach of these two books is to see harmony as an important part of real music. Each chapter has two sections, the first dealing with harmony, the second with melody. It is important to combine the study of harmony with melody for a number of reasons:

1. The study of melody, its shape, motives, sequences and climaxes, will help you understand patterns and shape in harmony.
2. A combined study of harmony and melody will help give meaning to music as a whole. This is important whether you enjoy music as a listener, a performer or a composer.
3. A knowledge of melodic flow and shape will mean that you see and hear harmony as much more than a series of chords strung together according to certain rules.
4. You will be working with the ingredients of music in a creative way.

Composing is important for all musicians, because it helps you to understand music from the inside. In English classes, you write creatively on many subjects. The same is true of art, domestic science, woodwork and physical education. Few people would stress the importance of theory and rules in these subjects before actively taking part in them. We all learn by doing, by taking part in the subject or game.

At the end of each half-chapter you will find some work to do. Tackle this in a musical and practical way. Always play and listen to the music examples – they all come from composed music: nothing has been written to prove a theoretical point. The music comes from the work of composers over many centuries, ranging from plainsong to the popular music of the present day. By hearing this wide range of music you will begin to understand how music, in its widest and truest sense, really works.

CHAPTER ONE

Writing for the piano: harmony

There are many different ways of using harmony, melody and rhythm when composing music for the piano. Here are some of the more usual piano styles.

Block chords

This style is rather like writing for voices in the choral style but there are three important differences to remember when writing for the piano.

1. The choral style generally has four voice parts (SATB) but piano chords can be written in any number of voices.

2. The number of notes in a chord can change from bar to bar adding interest to the music. This is called texture.

3. The piano has a wide range of notes – more than seven octaves. This range is much greater than that of the average four-part choir. Sounds can easily be varied from one register or pitch to another.

Play or listen to this well-known piece for piano. Notice that there are two- and three-note chords – these are chords of a thin texture. In contrast there are also chords of a thick texture with as many as nine notes in one single chord.

Chopin: Prelude in A, Op. 28 no. 7

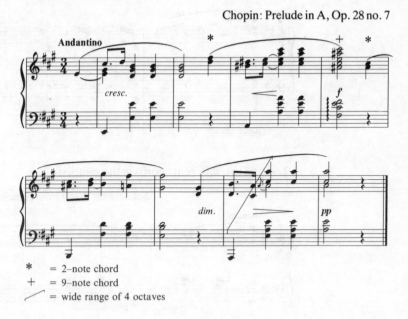

* = 2–note chord
+ = 9–note chord
◢ = wide range of 4 octaves

Leaping bass

The root or lowest note of a chord is sounded on the first beat of a bar; then other voices complete the chord on the following beats. The bass note can be held on by using the sustaining (right) pedal of the piano.

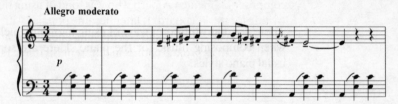

Grieg: Waltz from *Lyric Pieces*, Op. 12

The leaping bass style is popular in dance-like music such as the waltz, mazurka and ländler where there is often one chord to each bar.

The bass pattern is sometimes varied by:

1. changing to a block chord

Schubert: Scherzo in B flat, D 593 no.1

* = Block chord

2. using two different chords in the same bar

Schumann: Waltz from *Albumblätter*, Op. 124

⌐___ = Chord change

Alberti bass   The Alberti bass took its name from the 18th-century Italian
composer Domenico Alberti who was fond of using this style of
writing for the keyboard. It later became popular with composers
such as Haydn, Mozart and Beethoven. Chords are spread out by
playing them as broken chords in different rhythms. For example:

The broken chords in this example are written in close position.

Mozart: Piano Sonata in C, K 545 (1st movement)

Rolling bass   This style is rather like the Alberti bass, but composers of the 19th
century often preferred to use broken chords in a more open position.

Chopin: *Grand Studies*, Op. 10 no. 9

The rolling bass style sometimes uses broken chords spread over several octaves. The effect is rich and exciting.

Liszt: 'O Liebe' from *Liebesträume*

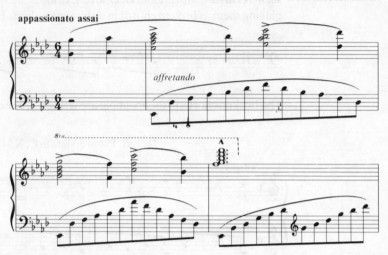

Alternating bass

This is similar to the leaping bass, but the alternating bass has a bass note at the start of each bar which changes between the root and the 5th or the root and the 3rd of the chord. This change of notes on alternate beats or alternate bars helps give variety and move the rhythm forwards.

Chopin: Waltz, Op. 64 no. 1

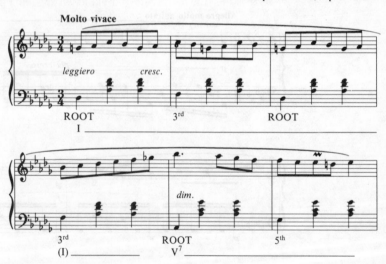

Texture   Play this chord in these different registers.

You will notice that the quality of its sound changes as you move
around the keyboard. Low bass-range chords have a thick, sometimes
muddy sound. High treble chords have a clear, sometimes thin sound.
Composers tend to avoid using close-position chords in the low
registers of the piano except for special effects. As a general rule, it
is better to write open-position chords in the bass and use
close-position only for the middle and high registers of the piano.

You can see this idea at work here:

Schumann: Allegro from *Carnival Jest from Vienna*, Op. 26

When the left hand is playing in the low register, notes of the chord
are widely spaced in open position. When the left hand moves to the
middle register of the keyboard, the chord notes are in close position.

To change the texture in your piano writing you may:

1. Move the chords to a different register.

Mozart: Piano Sonata in B flat (Trio)

└───┘ = Chords in a lower register

2. Vary the number of notes in a chord.

3. Reverse the parts by writing the melody for the left hand and the chords for the right hand. Sometimes the right hand crosses the left hand and plays the melody at a lower pitch.

4. Change the rhythm of the chords.

Grieg: Album Leaf from *Lyric Pieces*, Op. 12

Listen to this example and you will hear that the composer varies the number of notes in the left-hand chords (Method 2, bars 1–9). He also reverses the parts in bar 10 by moving the melody to the left hand (Method 3), and changes the rhythm of the chords which accompany the melody (Method 4).

WORK ON WRITING FOR THE PIANO: HARMONY

1. Play or listen to these extracts of piano writing then decide which of these styles is used for the accompaniment: block chord, leaping bass, alberti bass, rolling bass, alternating bass.

Chopin: *Grande valse brillante*, Op. 18

Mozart: Piano Sonata in C, K 545 (2nd movement)

Chopin: Waltz, Op. 64 no. 3

Chopin: Mazurka, Op. 68 no. 3

Chopin: Nocturne, Op. 27 no. 1

2. Comment on the texture of these pieces by listing the method or methods used in each case to vary the texture.

Schubert: Piano Sonata in A, D 664 (2nd movement)

1.

Beethoven: Piano Sonata in C, Op. 53 (1st movement)

2.

Mozart: Piano Sonata in C minor, K 457 (1st movement)

3.

Grieg: Scherzo-Impromptu from *Moods*, Op. 73 no. 2

4.

3. Write your own piano accompaniments for these melodies. Use a different accompaniment style for each. You may use the suggested openings, or make up your own.

Dussek: Sonatina in G, Op. 20 no. 1 (2nd movement)

1.

Mendelssohn: *Kinderstück* in G, Op. 72 no. 1

Brahms: Waltz, Op. 39 no. 5

Wallace: 'Scenes that are Brightest' from *Maritana*

4. Re-write your accompaniments from question 3 and change the texture of each. You may (a) move some chords to a different register, (b) vary the number of notes in each chord, (c) reverse the parts, or (d) change the rhythm of the chords, but use a different method for each accompaniment.

5. Compose your own piano piece of between 8 and 16 bars. Use any of the styles mentioned in Chapter 1.

Writing for the piano: melody

During the 17th century music began to change in a number of ways. One of these changes concerned the way composers thought of harmony and melody. Up to about 1600, harmony came from the weaving together of several different lines of melody. This style of music is called polyphony after the Greek words 'poly', which means many or several, and 'phoné', a voice. From 1600 onwards composers began to think more in terms of a single melody supported by its own harmony or accompaniment of chords. This meant that a melody was closely linked to chords, chord progressions and harmonic patterns.

If we take a simple chord it is quite easy to see this idea in practice. By writing the four notes of the chord in different orders and in different rhythms it is possible to compose a variety of motives or melodic ideas.

(a) Mozart: String Quintet in G minor, K 516 (1st movement)

(b) Mahler: Symphony No. 4 (4th movement)

(c) Wagner: Die Meistersinger von Nürnberg

We can take this idea one step further. By repeating certain notes of the chord and/or using the same notes at a different pitch it is possible to invent longer melodic ideas.

(a) Schubert: *Rosamunde*

(b) Beethoven: String Quartet Op. 18 no. 2 (3rd movement)

(c) Folk Song: 'Michael Finnigin'

(d) French folk song: 'As-tu vu la casquette?'

Composers often build up melodies for the piano by using simple chord patterns in one or more of these ways:

1. Simple broken chords with or without embellishments.

Beethoven: Piano Sonata in E flat, Op. 7 (3rd movement)

Mozart: Piano Sonata in B flat (4th movement)

2. Scale and arpeggio passages.

Mozart: Piano Sonata in B flat, K 570 (1st movement)

3. Turning patterns.

Mozart: Piano Sonata in C minor, K 457 (2nd movement)

4. Arpeggios over several octaves with or without embellishments.

Chopin: *Valse brillante*, Op. 34 no. 1

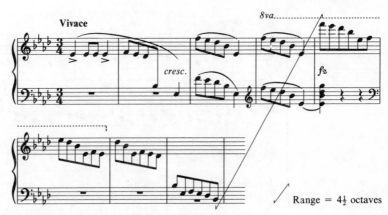

Range = 4½ octaves

WORK ON WRITING FOR THE PIANO: MELODY

1. a) Play or listen to these short sections from piano pieces.
   b) Say how the melody is built up from the chords.
   c) Write out the chord pattern for each.

Example:

Haydn: Piano Sonata in D, Hob. XVI no. 33 (Minuet)

The melody is built up from simple broken chords with embellishments.

Mozart: Piano Sonata in C, K 309 (3rd movement)

Mozart: Piano Sonata in D, K 576 (1st movement)

Beethoven: Piano Sonata in A, Op. 2 no. 2 (last movement)

Beethoven: Piano Sonata in E flat, Op. 31 no. 3 (1st movement)

(combination of 3 methods)

Müller: Menuetto

(combination of 3 methods)

5.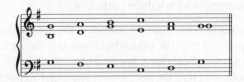

2. Compose four separate phrases (each of 4 to 8 bars) to show the different ways of building up a melody from this chord pattern.

3. a) Write a progression of eight chords ending with a perfect cadence.
   b) Compose a short motive in the same key as the chord pattern.
   c) Develop your motive into a phrase of between 8 and 16 bars long based on the chord pattern.
   d) Use one or more of these ideas in your melody: broken chords, scale and arpeggio passages, turning figures, arpeggios over two or more octaves.
   e) Embellish the melody if and where appropriate.
   f) Add phrase marks, tempo and expression.

CHAPTER TWO

Suspensions and pedal points

Suspensions and pedal points are embellishments (see *Harmony, Melody and Composition*: Chapter 6).

Suspensions

A suspension occurs when changing chords. One note is left sounding when the chord changes. This delayed movement in one of the parts affects both the harmony and the rhythm. It produces a clash or tension in the harmony and a delay in the rhythm. When the held-over note moves to a note of the new chord, the tension is relieved.

All suspensions have three parts:

1. Preparation (P): the appearance of the note in the first chord.
2. Suspension (S): the note is held over into the next chord, which falls on a strong beat (see Chapter 3).
3. Resolution (R): the note moves one step to a note of the new chord.

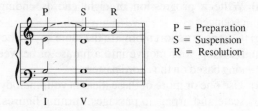

P = Preparation
S = Suspension
R = Resolution

Suspensions have been used in music since the 14th century. They have since become among the most expressive of all embellishments.

Byrd: motet *Ave verum corpus*

Tchaikovsky: Symphony No. 6, 'The Pathetic' (4th movement)

Suspensions in
upper parts

Suspensions in an upper part (S, A or T) are known by the interval which they form above the bass note. There are four types:

(To be exact, the interval between soprano and bass in (a) is a 16th, but the suspension is always described as 9–8, not 16–15.)

Play the above examples and you will hear that some suspensions sound more clashing or dissonant than others. The effect of each suspension can be seen in this table.

Minor 9–8	Strong clash
Major 7–6	Strong clash
Major 9–8	Medium clash
Minor 7–6	Medium clash
Diminished 4–3	Medium clash
Perfect 4–3	*Mild clash
Major 6–5	Mild clash
Minor 6–5	Mild clash
* = stronger in 4-part writing	

Compare the effect of the two suspensions in this example. The 4–3 suspension is more gentle than the strong clash of the major 7–6 suspension which follows it in the next bar.

Vivaldi: *Gloria*

When a 4 – 3 suspension occurs in four-part writing the effect is a stronger clash because of the interval of a 7th between the soprano and tenor parts.

Bourgeois: Psalm No. 1

Suspensions in the lowest part are known by the interval which they form with the nearest part above. There are four types which usually move down by step.

As with suspensions in upper voices, the more dissonant the interval the more striking the suspension. For example, 2nds and 9ths make a stronger clash than 4ths or 5ths. Listen to the strong effect of 2 moving to 3 and compare this with the more gentle clash of 4 moving to 5.

Schütz: *St Luke Passion*

Mundy: anthem 'Rejoice in the Lord'

Notice these points about suspensions:

1. The held over (suspended) note is always placed on a strong or accented beat. It resolves on a weak beat.
2. Suspensions can occur in any part. Here is an example of a suspension in the bass voice.

Gibbons: First strain of song 46

3. It is best not to sound the note the suspension will resolve on to (R) in another part, against the suspended note. To do this would destroy the effect of the suspension as you can hear in this example.

There is one exception to this. Composers sometimes use the resolution note in the bass when the suspension is 9–8. The wide gap of a 9th makes the sound less harsh.

Purcell: *The Fairy Queen*

C major

4. Suspensions were first used according to very precise rules (strict suspensions). But after 1700 or so composers began to break away from these restrictions (free suspensions).

Strict suspensions (1400–1700)	Free suspensions (1700–present day)
1. The preparation note should be as long or longer than the suspended note.	1. The preparation note is sometimes shorter than the suspended note.
2. The suspended note is tied to the preparation.	2. The suspended note is sometimes sounded rather than tied.
3. The suspended note resolves downwards.	3. The suspended note may resolve up or down.

The suspension series

Several suspensions are linked together in a sequence pattern to form a series of suspensions. The resolution note becomes another suspension and so on, driving the music forwards.

Handel: Gigue from *Xerxes*

Double and triple suspensions

Suspensions are often heard in two or more parts at the same time. In this example there are several double suspensions where two notes are suspended or held over.

Bach: Prelude in F minor from *The Well-tempered Clavier*, Book 2

You will often hear triple suspensions in the music of Mozart, Haydn and Beethoven. Triple suspensions are sometimes called suspension chords because the chord V^7 is suspended over a tonic bass.

Mozart: *The Magic Flute*

The suspended leading note sometimes resolves upwards by step as can be seen in the melody.

Decorated
suspensions

A suspended note can move (a) to another note, or (b) to a decorated pattern before resolving.

Play these examples.

Brahms: Symphony No. 4 (2nd movement)

Bach: Organ Fugue in C minor

Pedal point

A note is held or repeated, usually in the bass, while chords change above or around it. Pedal points are like drones (which imitate the drone of a bagpipe).

Pedal points:

1. Often start and end as chord notes but have discordant passages in between.

Bach: Fugue in C minor from *The Well-tempered Clavier*, Book 1

⌐⎯⎯⌐ = pedal point

2. The pedal note is usually the tonic or dominant. Composers occasionally use other pedal notes such as the sub-dominant.

Tchaikovsky: Symphony No. 5 (2nd movement)

⌞___⌟ = pedal point on IV

3. The pedal note is sometimes repeated rather than held on (see example under **2**).

4. Pedal notes may be decorated with appoggiaturas or broken chord patterns.

Beethoven: Piano Sonata in C, Op. 2 no. 3 (Scherzo)

⌞___⌟ = pedal point on G with decoration

5. Pedal notes sometimes occur in a part other than the bass – these are called inverted pedals.

Bach: Fugue in G minor from *The Well-tempered Clavier*, Book 2

⌐___⌐ = inverted pedal

6. When both tonic and dominant are sounded together as pedal notes this is called a double pedal.

Grieg: Norwegian Melody from *Lyric Pieces*, Op. 12

⎣____⎦ = Double pedal

WORK ON SUSPENSIONS AND PEDAL POINTS

1. Copy out these extracts and play them through several times.
Analyse the suspensions (marked with an asterisk) by answering these
questions.

a) What is the type of suspension?
b) Does the suspension make a strong, medium or mild clash?
c) Is the suspension in an upper or lower voice?
d) Where do the different parts of the suspension occur in the music?

Mark on your copy a P for the preparation, S for the suspension and
R for the resolution.

Example:

Byrd: Mass in Four Parts (Kyrie)

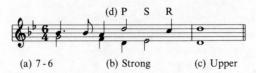

Pergolesi: *Stabat mater*

1.

* = Suspension

Handel: *Jephtha*

2.

* = Suspension

Byrd: *The Carmans Whistle* (Variation VI)

3.

* = Suspension

Bach: Prelude in A minor from *The Well-tempered Clavier*, Book 2

∗ = Suspension

2. Identify the suspensions in these examples as either (a) double, (b) triple, (c) a series of suspensions, (d) decorated, or (e) a suspension resolving upwards.

Bach: Italian Concerto (1st movement)

J. C. Bach: Piano Sonata in C minor, Op. 5 no. 6 (3rd movement)

Bach: Organ Prelude in E minor, BWV 548

J. C. Bach: Piano Sonata in C minor, Op. 5 no. 6 (2nd movement)

Haydn: Piano Sonata in E flat, Hob. XVI no. 49 (slow movement)

3. This extract includes 9–8, 7–6, 4–3 suspensions and a double suspension. Re-write the passage as simple harmony by removing all the suspensions.

Handel: *Messiah*

4. Complete the soprano of this two-part motet by writing a series of 7–6 suspensions. The first suspension has been included as a guide. Continue in the same rhythm and falling pattern.

Lassus: Motet *expectatio justorum*

(continue)

5. Add a soprano part in crotchet beats to this bass. Introduce suspensions as and where marked.

(continue)

9 - 8   4 - 3   9 - 8   4 - 3   9 - 8   4 - 3   9 - 8

6. Embellish this chord pattern by adding a double suspension at each asterisk. Follow the pattern set up at the start.

Bach: Prelude in F minor from *The Well-tempered Clavier*, Book 2

(continue)

* = Double suspension required

Compare your answer with the original – Prelude in F minor from Bach's *Well-tempered Clavier*, Book 2.

7. Re-write exercise **5** for SATB adding harmony for the inside parts (alto and tenor).

8. Add soprano, alto and tenor parts to these bass suspensions.

9. Write these chord progressions for SATB. Add a suspension at the asterisk in the part indicated. Play through your answers.

Chord pattern	*Key*	*Type of suspension*	*Suspension in*
I⁶ İV I⁶₄ V⁷ I	D major	9–8	Soprano
I⁶ İV I	A minor	9–8	Alto
VI İI V I	B flat major	9–8	Tenor
I⁶ V̇ I	E minor	4–3	Soprano
IV İ II VI İI⁶ V⁷ I	A flat major	4–3	Alto
II V̇I V⁶ I	C major	6–5	Tenor

10. Compose four chord progressions similar to those in exercise **9** to illustrate these suspensions in the lower part (write for SATB). Use a different key for each: (a) 2–3 (b) 4–5 (c) 5–6 (d) 9–10. ▸
Example:

11. Select four chord patterns from exercise 9 and decorate each suspension in a different way. There are some suggestions in the first part of this chapter if you get stuck for ideas.

12. Compose an 8-bar chord progression for SATB in a key of your choice. The chords in bars 1–2 should be above a tonic pedal note in the bass. The chords in bars 3–4 should be around a dominant pedal note in another part (an inverted pedal). The chords in bars 6–8 should be above a tonic pedal note in the bass.
The pedal notes should start and end as chord notes, but use dissonant chords in between.

Words and music

The human voice is one of the most expressive and flexible of all
melodic instruments. It usually performs words with music, so it is
important to know something about the close bond between words
and music.

Words can affect the music a composer writes in a number of ways.
Both words and music have rhythm, pitch, form and meaning. By
highlighting the style of a piece of prose or poetry a composer can add
new meaning to the words through his music.

**The influence
of words on
rhythm**

Words can influence melodic rhythm in a number of ways:
1. Metre and melodic rhythm. Metre is the rhythm of poetry. It
includes:
a) the number of lines in a verse
b) the number of syllables in each line
c) the accents of words and syllables.

A great deal of the music composed in Europe during the 17th, 18th
and 19th centuries is written in *bars* of equal time length. Traditional
poetry also has equal time lengths – these are called *feet. Prosody* (the
correct setting of word accents to music) means that the metre of the
melody tends to follow the metre of the words. In both words and
music there is an accent every two or three sounds. In four or more
syllables or notes there are two or more accents. For example:

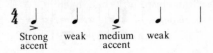

Strong   weak   medium   weak
accent   accent

These are the five most common patterns of accents (∪ = weak;
— =strong).

Accent patterns (Name of metre)	Example of poetry	Some musical equivalents and examples
strong weak — ∪ (Trochaic)	Jack and Jill went up — ∪ — ∪ — the hill ∪ —	$\frac{3}{4}$ 𝅗𝅥 ♩ 𝅘𝅥 │𝅗𝅥 ♩ 𝅘𝅥 ‖ or $\frac{6}{8}$ ♩ ♪♩ ♪│ For example: Sum - mer is i - cum - en in — ∪ — ∪ — ∪ —

Accent patterns (Name of metre)	Example of poetry	Some musical equivalents and examples
weak strong ◡ — (Iambic)	I wandered lonely as ◡ — ◡ — ◡ — a cloud ◡ —	3/4 ♩♪|♩♪|♩♪ or 6/8 ♪♩|♪♩ or 4/4 ♩♩|♩♩♩|♩ For example: O God our help in a-ges past ◡ — ◡ — ◡ — ◡ —
strong weak weak — ◡ ◡ (Dactylic)	Take her up tenderly — ◡ ◡ — ◡ ◡	4/4 ♩ ♪♪|♩ ♪♪ ‖ or 2/4 ♪ ♪♪|♪ ♪♪ ‖ or 3/4 ♩ ♩ ♩ ‖ or ♩. ♪♪ ‖ For example: God save our gra - cious Queen — ◡ ◡
weak strong weak ◡ — ◡ (Amphibrachic)	The dull ass is braying ◡ — ◡ ◡ ◡ — ◡ the black horse is ◡ — ◡ neighing — ◡	4/4 ♪|♩ ♪♪|♩ ♪ or 2/4 ♪|♩ ♪♪|♩ ♪ For example: Brahms: Academic Festival Overture ◡ — ◡ ◡ — ◡ ◡ — ◡ ◡ —
weak weak strong ◡ ◡ — (Anapaestic)	There are hills beyond ◡ ◡ — ◡ Pentland and lands — ◡ ◡ — beyond Forth ◡ ◡ —	4/4 ♪♪|♩ ♪♪|♩ or 2/4 ♪♪|♩ ♪♪|♩ or 4/4 ♪.♪|♩ ♪.♪|♩ ♪.♪ For example: Loch Lomond Oh and ye'll tak' the high road and I'll tak' the low

2. Words and syllables have their own accents and these are often matched up with musical accents. Less important words such as 'a', 'up', 'to', 'it' do not have musical accents.

With words of two syllables, one syllable is always accented more than the other. Say the words 'although' and 'agree'. You will hear that the accent comes on the second syllable in each case:

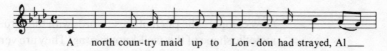

al-though   a-gree

Try saying the two words again but with accents on their first syllables. The accents are misplaced and sound quite wrong.

Sing through the beginning of this folk song and you will notice these points illustrated in the musical setting of the words.

Folk song: 'The Oak and the Ash'

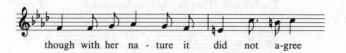

A   north coun-try maid up to Lon - don had strayed, Al___

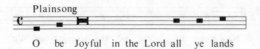

though with her na - ture it   did   not   a-gree

3. In religious chanting and recitative the rhythm of the words is more like dramatic speech than sung melody. (Recitative is a style of singing in speech rhythm and is heard in opera and oratorio.) Often the rhythm is not written in note values and the singer(s) performs the natural rhythm of the words to a single note.

Plainsong

O be Joyful in the Lord all ye lands

Recitative   Evangelist   Schütz: *St Luke Passion*

And he co-meth un-to the di - sci - ples, and fin-deth them a - sleep

The subject of words and music is both fascinating and involved. Metre and melodic rhythm were not so closely related in music of the 13th to 16th centuries. Composers of the 20th century have looked for new ways of using metre and melodic rhythm. Stravinsky, for example, used two or more metric patterns together to great effect. All this is beyond the scope of this book, but a study of metre and rhythm in 20th-century music, folk song or rock music would prove rewarding for those of you who are interested in this topic.

Words and melodic shape

Each language has its own special characteristics. English, for example, has more strong accents than French. Chinese is a difficult language to learn because you can give the same word different meanings just by changing the pitch of your voice. Changing the pitch of your voice when speaking is called *inflection*.

1. Spoken inflection can suggest shape and pitch in melody writing.

Important words often use higher notes as well as coming on strong accents. You can hear this quite clearly in this simple illustration. Say the words 'There's a hole in my bucket' and you will notice that there is pitch as well as rhythm in your speech. The pitch of voice will probably be something like this:

Now compare the pitch of these words with the actual notes and melodic shape of this well-known song. They are very similar.

Traditional: 'There's a hole in my bucket'

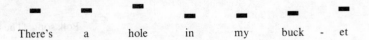

This striking melody by Bach gradually rises as the words become stronger and more important. There is an octave leap on the word 'might' and this leads to a grand climax on 'God'.

Bach: cantata no. 50

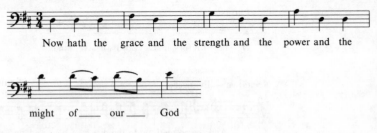

2. Words can also influence melody by their meanings.

A simple example is the call of the cuckoo in this folk song.

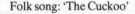
Folk song: 'The Cuckoo'

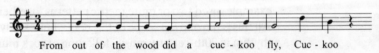

or the 'tick-tock' of a clock:

Traditional: 'My Grandfather's Clock'

tick - tock   tick - tock

Composers often illustrate the meanings of words in musical images, for example the blowing with the wind:

Handel: *Israel in Egypt*

Thou didst blow _____ with the wind,

or this trumpet-like fanfare:

Walton: *Belshazzar's Feast*

Blow   up   the   trum - pet,

From the same work there are two different musical images for the word 'fallen':

Walton: *Belshazzar's Feast*

fall - en,   fall_____ en,

There are many similar examples. Haydn (in *The Creation*) and Handel (in *Israel in Egypt*) both illustrate lightning, thunder and rain with musical images. Handel even has locusts, flies and jumping frogs with music of a similar descriptive quality. In the chorus 'He sent a thick darkness over all the land' the music is slow, uses many flats and the voice parts stay low in pitch.

Note:
You have seen a few of the ways in which words can influence the kind of music composers write. But this is a two-way process. Music has its own form and style. Music, with its own special patterns and requirements, can and does influence words. Composers of popular music often admit to writing the music before the words. There is no

doubt that composers of vocal and choral music such as Mozart and Schubert are influenced by the words they set to music, but their music also works as music in its own right.

Practical hints for setting words to music

1. Each syllable should be written exactly under its appropriate note or notes. This means that notes are usually spaced wider apart to avoid cramping words together.
2. Keep inside the range of the singers' voices.
3. Avoid awkward leaps and intervals.
4. Syllabic word setting is where each syllable has a separate sound.

Handel: *Messiah*

The migh-ty God.   The Ev-er-last-ing Fa-ther

Notes are written separately, even if they belong to the same beat.

5. Melismatic setting is where two or more notes are written for one word or syllable. The notes are grouped in beats with a slur over them.

Handel: *Messiah*

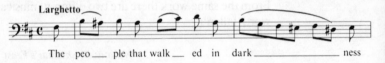

The   peo __ ple that walk __ ed in   dark _____ ness

6. Divide words into separate syllables correctly. For example:

to-geth-er	not	tog-e-ther
ne-ver	not	nev-er
with-out	not	wi-thout
tall-er	not	tal-ler
sor-row	not	sorr-ow

This can be a problem as you can see in the last two examples. There are no clear rules. A knowledge of grammar (prefixes, suffixes, consonants, vowels, diphthongs) will help here. Look at songs to see how syllables are divided and you will soon get the idea.

7. The style of words can often suggest a style for your melodies –
fast, spiky, repetitive, delicate, slow, peaceful, smooth, bright, are
just a few of the qualities heard in poetry and music. Some words will
suggest leaps in music, others will need a melody which moves
smoothly by step.

8. When setting words for several voices (for example, SATB)
remember that the voices may enter at different points in the music.
This means that they will end at different times unless you use one or
more of these ideas to allow parts to catch up.
a) repeat certain words or phrases
b) long notes
c) several notes to one syllable or word
d) rests
e) leave out certain words, so long as the words still make sense.

WORK ON WORDS AND MUSIC

1. a) Divide these words into syllables: pretending, forsaken,
undeserving, revolution, messenger, simplicity, rejoicing,
glittering, quietness, celebrate, whosoever, harmonious,
international, Constantinople, possibility.
b) Indicate the accented and unaccented syllables by writing the
prosody signs under each syllable (— = strong ∪ = weak).
c) Set each word to appropriate music.

Example: Mer-ri-ly

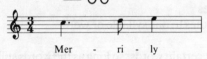

2. Compose a melody for these words in recitative style. This style of
singing follows the natural, free rhythm of the words as if you were
speaking them:

'I have found among my papers a sheet in which I call architecture
frozen music' (Goethe).

3. Compose melodies for these words. Match the musical accents in
your settings to the accents of the words.

Round and round the rugged rock
The ragged rascal ran,
How many R's are there in that?
Now tell me if you can.
                    (Anon.)

There were three Ravens sat on a tree,
They were as black as black might be.
The one of them said to his mate,
'Where shall we our breakfast take?'
                    (Traditional)

4. Set these words to music. Try to make your melody echo the
meaning of the words by using musical images.

Cuckoo, cuckoo, cherry tree,
Catch a bird, and give it to me;
Let the tree be high or low,
Let it hail or rain or snow.
                    (Anon.)

A milk white bird
Floats down through the air.
And never a tree
But he lights there.
                    (Anon.)

CHAPTER THREE

Seventh chords

Seventh chords may be built on any degree of the major or minor scale. You have already looked at the most important seventh chord, the dominant 7th, in *Harmony, Melody and Composition* (Chapter 13). Other seventh chords are called secondary sevenths. They are:

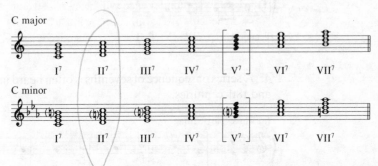

C major

I⁷ II⁷ III⁷ IV⁷ ⌊V⁷⌋ VI⁷ VII⁷

C minor

I⁷ II⁷ III⁷ IV⁷ ⌊V⁷⌋ VI⁷ VII⁷

Secondary seventh chords in minor keys can use notes from either the harmonic or the melodic minor scale.

Uses of seventh chords

1. To make rich and colourful harmony.

Bach: chorale *Mit Fried' und Freud' ich fahr' dahin*

C major: III⁷   VI⁷   V ⁷   IV ⁷   III⁷   (G major)

2. Sevenths are bright, active chords and they help to move the harmony forwards.

Ravel: *Pavane pour une Infante défunte*

(IV⁷) II⁷_____ V⁷_____I⁷_____ IV⁷_____VII⁷_____

( ) = not part of the chord

3. To push the music forward to a cadence.

Bach: chorale *Vater unser im Himmelreich*

(F major)   IV⁷   V ⁽⁷⁾ I

4. A series or sequence of sevenths is often heard in music of the 17th and 18th centuries.

(a) Three–part writing

II⁷   V⁷   I⁷   IV⁷   VII⁷ III⁷ VI⁷   II⁷   V⁷

(b) Four–part writing

II⁷   V⁷   I⁷   IV⁷   VII⁷ III⁷ VI⁷   II⁷   V⁷

Bach: Passacaglia and Fugue in C minor for organ

(c)

(B♭ major) VI⁷   II⁷   V⁷   I⁷   IV⁷ G minor: II⁷   V⁷

Notice that:
a) root movements either rise a 4th or fall a 5th.
b) In three-part writing the 5th of each chord is left out. In four parts the 5th is left out in alternate chords and the root is doubled. This avoids parallels.
c) The 7th of one chord moves down to the 3rd of the next chord, and this 3rd becomes the 7th of the following chord.

5. Seventh chords can also help music to move through different keys.

Bach: Fugue in C minor from *The Well-tempered Clavier*, Book 2

C minor ____ A♭ major ____ F minor _____

Before secondary sevenths were thought of as chords they occurred as suspensions in 16th-century choral music.

Amner: anthem 'Lift up your heads, O ye gates'

The chord marked with an asterisk could be described a II⁷ or as VII⁶ with the G suspended. This explains why the 7th of a seventh chord is often 'prepared' as in a suspension.

Movement to the 7th of secondary seventh chords

1. The dissonant 7th is often prepared by sounding this note first in another chord in the same voice.

Bach: *St John Passion*

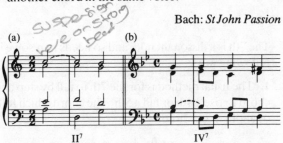

(There is an important difference between a suspension and a secondary seventh chord. A suspension is sounded on a strong beat, but a secondary seventh can be written on either a strong or a weak beat.)

2. The 7th can be approached by step.

I⁷

Spiritual: 'Were you there?'

Some-times   it   caus-es me to   trem-ble, trem-ble, trem-ble

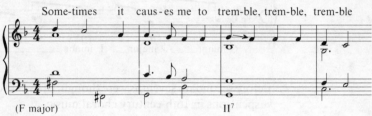

(F major)   II⁷

3. The 7th can also be approached by a leap from another note. (The 5th of the chord, for example, can leap to the 7th then move inside the leap.)

VI⁷

Spiritual: 'Balm in Gilead'

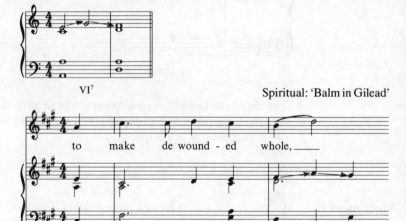

to   make   de wound - ed   whole, ____

II⁷

Resolving seventh chords

The 7th is a dissonant note and so needs to resolve in one of the following ways:

1. The usual method is for the 7th to fall by step and the root of the chord to rise a 4th or fall a 5th. The chord which follows may be a triad or another 7th chord.

II⁷   V   II⁷   V⁷

or

2. The 7th falls by step and the root rises by step.

III⁷   IV

3. The 7th falls by step and the root stays on the same note.

IV⁷   II₅⁶   V   I

Like V⁷ the 7th of other seventh chords can be decorated, move to another voice, or be delayed before resolving.

Bach: Prelude in F from *Six Little Preludes*, BWV 933–8

(C major)   IV⁷

⌒⟶ = 7ᵗʰ delayed resolution

Bridge: 'Heart's Ease' from *Two Lyrics*

VI⁷

○ = 7ᵗʰ changing to another voice

Corelli: Trio Sonata in E, Op. 4 no. 6 (Gigue)

VI⁷   II⁷   V⁷   I⁷   IV⁷

○ = 7ᵗʰˢ alternating between voices

Inversions of seventh chords

Like the dominant seventh, other seventh chords have three inversions. Their figuring is always the same:

I⁷ of C major with inversions

Movement to and from the 7th in inversions

Inversions of seventh chords are prepared and resolved like those of V⁷.

1. The 7th of the chord (whether in S, A, T or B) is usually prepared in the same part.

Dale: hymn-tune 'St Catherine'

2. The 7th generally resolves downwards by step.

Franck: *Prelude, Chorale and Fugue* for piano (Chorale)

3. The 7th may stay in the same part while other voices move to another triad.

14th-century German carol: *In dulci jubilo*

II⁷ in cadences

Apart from V⁷, II⁷ is one of the most useful of all seventh chords. It is often heard at cadence points.

Purcell: *King Arthur*

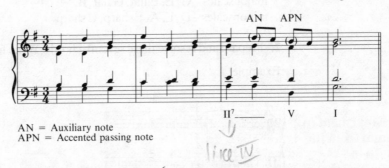

AN = Auxiliary note
APN = Accented passing note

The first inversion of II⁷ (II $\frac{6}{5}$) is sometimes called the 'chord of the added 6th' because it looks like chord IV with a 6th added above the bass. Bach often used this chord just before a perfect or interrupted cadence.

Bach: cantata no. 78

WORK ON SEVENTH CHORDS

1. Write, play and sing seventh chords on each degree of these scales:
major scales – G, E, E flat, G flat, B
minor scales – D, F, A, F sharp, C sharp

2. Prepare and resolve these seventh chords. Write for SATB.

Example:

P = Preparation
R = Resolution

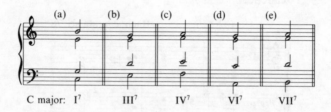

C major: I⁷   III⁷   IV⁷   VI⁷   VII⁷

3. Prepare and resolve these seventh chords for SAB.

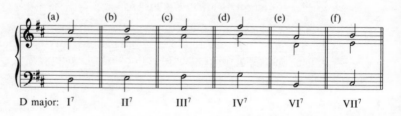

D major: I⁷   II⁷   III⁷   IV⁷   VI⁷   VII⁷

4. Complete the following progressions for SATB which include
seventh chords in some of their different minor forms. (Prepare the
7th in the previous chord or move to it downwards by step.)

Example:

I⁶   I⁷   IV   V

C minor: I II⁷ III IV V V⁶ I III⁷IV V I I IV⁷ V⁷ VI I VI⁷ V⁶₅ I

5. Write three separate progressions, each of four chords,

a) to show how the root of a seventh chord moves down a 5th (A major)

b) to show how the root of a seventh chord rises by step (B flat major)

c) to show how the root of a seventh chord stays on the same note (E minor)

6. Compose a sequence/series of seventh chords in D major for SATB. Use the given opening and continue this pattern until you arrive at chord I again.

D major: I   VI⁷   II⁷   V⁷

7. Play the sequence of seventh chords (exercise 5) in several different major and minor keys.

8. Decorate your sequence of seventh chords in three different ways. You may use (a) broken chord patterns (b) passing notes (c) auxiliary notes, or other ideas of your own, for example:

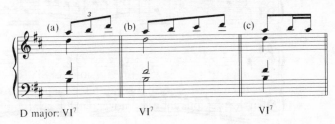

D major: VI⁷   VI⁷   VI⁷

9. Write in F major the three inversions of each seventh chord of the key. Figure each chord. Play and sing your answers.

10. Compose a piece for piano of about 16 bars.

a) use a variety of seventh chords in root position and inversions together with other chords

b) approach and leave the 7th in a number of different ways

c) end your piece with a decorated II⁶₅–V–I cadence.

Writing for the piano: accompaniments to songs

The piano was invented around 1710, but true piano music appeared only after the 1750s. Much of the music composed for earlier keyboard instruments (for example, harpsichord, clavichord, virginals) is often played on the piano today. The history of keyboard music goes back 500 years and can be divided into five broad periods and styles.

16th century

16th-century keyboard music represents the early style of keyboard music. The main points to notice are:
1. Fast scales up and down the keyboard.
2. Arpeggios.
3. Fast repeated chords.
4. Repeated patterns of broken chords.
5. Repeated patterns of 3rds.
6. Embellishments (trills, mordents, etc.).

Bull: The Kings Hunting Jigg

Forms

1. Variations on popular tunes.
2. Ground bass – a bass line is repeated throughout a piece as a foundation for melodic, harmonic and contrapuntal variations.
3. Dances – galliards, pavans, allemandes.
4. Pieces with descriptive titles – e.g. 'The Kings Juell', 'The Carmans Whistle', 'The Queens Command'.
5. Preludes.

Composers   England: Giles Farnaby, William Byrd, John Bull, Orlando Gibbons. The main collections of their pieces are *Parthenia* (the first published collection of English virginal music), *The Fitzwilliam Virginal Book*, and *My Lady Nevells Book* (42 pieces by Byrd).

Baroque

The main points of style to notice in the Baroque period (late 17th and early 18th centuries) are:

1. Contrapuntal texture. This is the art of continuing two or more individual melodic lines together. Imitation, sequence and inversion are all used to help make the music interesting.

Bach: Two-part Invention no. 1

2. A more chordal style was sometimes used with cadenza passages (a cadenza is a showy and ornamental section of writing).

Bach: Chromatic Fantasy

Forms   **1.** Inventions.
2. Preludes and fugues.
3. Sonatas.
4. The suite – groups of dances such as the allemande, courante, sarabande and gigue.
5. Variation forms – chaconne, passacaglia and ground bass.
6. Toccata and fantasia.

Composers   Couperin, Rameau, Bach, Domenico Scarlatti, Purcell, Handel.

Classical   Composers of the Classical period (1750–1830) were much more
                     interested in the piano than the older keyboard instruments. The
                     main points of style to notice are:

1. Melodies were more compact, clear and simple compared to the
long melodic lines and ornate figures of the early 18th century.
Phrases are often shorter, more symmetrical and very clear.

2. Counterpoint was still used but became less important.

3. The homophonic style, where a single melody is supported with
chords, began to appear.

4. Harmony is more direct, simple, often using only primary and
secondary triads, and a few seventh chords.

5. Dynamics – classical composers paid careful attention to dynamics:
louds, softs, general shading (*crescendo* and *diminuendo*).

Haydn: Piano Sonata in F, Hob. XVI:29 (1st movement)

6. Beethoven's piano music is more intense and dramatic with
sudden changes of emotion. He uses heavy, thick chords in the low
register of the piano, long chromatic scales, 3rds in contrary motion
and widely-spaced hands.

Beethoven: Piano Sonata in F minor, 'The Appassionata', Op. 57
(1st movement)

Forms
1. The keyboard sonata (in two, three or four movements).
2. First-movement sonata form.
3. Rondo.
4. Variations.
5. Minuet and trio.
6. Scherzo.
7. Sonatina.

Composers   Mozart, Haydn, Beethoven, Schubert.

Romantic

The 19th century (Romantic period) saw important developments in the piano. Improvements to the mechanism developed alongside new demands made by the music composers wrote for the instrument. The pianist-composer used the damper (sustaining) pedal for greater sound and warmth of tone.

Rich harmony, chromatic passages, mixed harmonies and difficult technical passages all occur in piano music at this time.

Chopin: Nocturne, Op. 9 no. 2

Forms   Shorter pieces were most common.
                   1. Dances – waltz, polonaise.
                   2. Nocturne.
                   3. Romanza.
                   4. Fantasy.
                   5. Ballade.
                   6. Étude.
                   7. Variation form.

Composers   Schumann, Mendelssohn, Chopin, Liszt, Brahms, Grieg, Albeniz,
                   Fauré, MacDowell, Granados, Busoni.

20th century   It is impossible to mention more than just a few of the many different
                   styles and composers of 20th-century piano music. Of special interest
                   is the music of:
                   1. Scriabin (Sonatas and Preludes). Scriabin devised a 'mystic chord'
                   using notes from the harmonic series (see *Harmony, Melody and
                   Composition*: Chapter 3) built up in 4ths.

numbers in the
Harmonic Series

2. Debussy (*Préludes, Arabesques, Images, Children's Corner Suite,
Suite Bergamasque*). Debussy developed a very original style of
composing inspired by the French Impressionist painters and writers.
His music uses:
a) the old modes and pentatonic scale (see *Harmony, Melody and
   Composition*: Chapter 5)
b) scales made up from whole tones
c) chords of open 5ths and octaves
d) parallel chord movement
e) free rhythms with less regular bar lines
f) flowing melody
g) widely-spaced hands and the extreme ranges of the piano

Debussy: 'La cathédrale engloutie' from *Préludes*, Book 1

3. Bartók (*Mikrokosmos, Allegro barbaro, Out of Doors, Bagatelles*). Bartók's piano music uses Hungarian folk music, counterpoint and chord passages, exciting rhythms, short melodic patterns and dissonant harmony.

Bartók: Scherzo from *Mikrokosmos*, Vol. 3

You should also look at the piano music of Ravel, Satie and Shostakovich. When studying the styles used in keyboard writing, look for differences in melody, harmony, form and keyboard technique. Try to identify the different styles by ear as well as by eye before you attempt to use them in your own writing.

Piano accompaniments to songs

Here are eight of the most common styles of piano accompaniment.

1. The right hand follows the vocal line. The left and/or right hand fills in the harmony.

Brahms: 'Schön war, das ich dir weihte', Op. 95 no.7

2. The piano part supplies music for only some of the melodic notes.

Wolf: 'Das verlassene Mägdlein' ('The forsaken maiden') from *Mörike-Lieder*

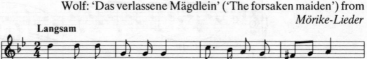

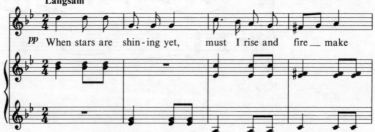

3. The sung melody moves around independently while the piano
supports the vocal line with held chords.

Tchaikovsky: song 'Warum nur', Op. 16 no. 5

With   laugh - ter   thou   fol - low - est   me,_____

4. The piano plays repeated chords under or around the vocal
melody.

Britten: Sonnet no. 30 from *Seven Sonnets of Michelangelo*

Veg-gio co'   bei___   vo - stri oc-chi un dol-ce   lu - me,___

5. The piano has flowing broken chord patterns.

Wolf: 'Auch kleine Dinge' ('E'en little things')

E'en lit - tle things   may   oft - en give us plea - sure,

6. The piano provides a harmonic background by playing arpeggios.

Sturman: Summer from *Seasons*

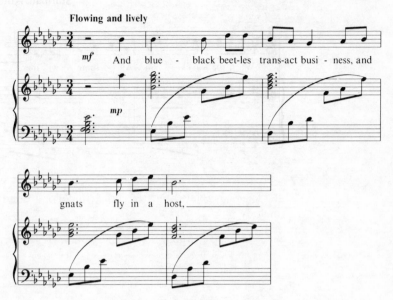

7. The piano introduces the mood of the song.

Schumann: *Die beiden Grenadiere* ('The two grenadiers'), Op. 49

8. The piano has its own melody in a kind of musical conversation with the voice.

Sturman: Autumn from *Seasons*

When the leaves   in Au - tumn wi - ther,_____ with a

WORK ON WRITING FOR THE KEYBOARD AND PIANO ACCOMPANIMENTS

1. Select three keyboard pieces from each of the five periods mentioned in the chapter.

Study each work in these ways:
a) look carefully through the music
b) listen to the music several times
c) play the music through if you are able to do so.

As you look, listen and play, try to become aware of the individual styles. It will help to look at the harmony, melody, form and keyboard style of each piece. The information in the chapter is of a very general nature. It can only guide you in the right direction. Composers are individuals and their music does not fit neatly into compartments with labels. Even the same composer will write differently at different times in his life.

With practice you should be able to identify contrasting styles of keyboard music by ear as well as by eye.

You may then feel able to imitate these styles in your writing. Start perhaps with a Bach two-part invention as a model. See what you can set down on paper or improvise at the keyboard.

2. Name the way in which the piano is accompanying in these extracts. (Refer to the eight most common styles of accompaniment described in the chapter.)

R. Strauss: 'Ruhe, meine Seele!' (Rest, my soul'), Op. 27 no. 1

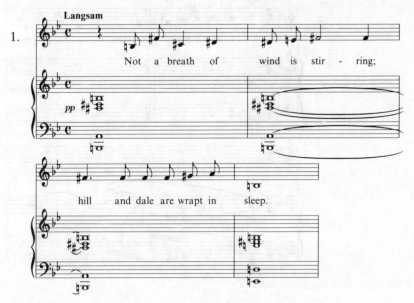

Grieg: *Margaret's Cradle Song*, Op. 15 no. 1

Tchaikovsky: 'The veil of night has fallen', Op. 47 no. 3

R. Strauss: 'O wärst du mein' ('O wert thou mine'), Op. 26 no. 2

Tchaikovsky: 'Tell me, why are roses so pale?', Op. 6 no. 5

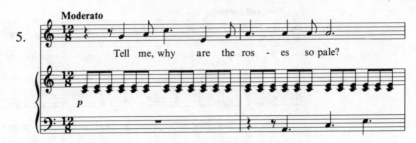

3. Write your own piano accompaniments to these three melodies. Use at least two but no more than four of the different styles of accompaniment in each song.

Look again at Chapter 1 to remind yourself of the ways in which harmony, melody and rhythm are used in piano writing.

Traditional Neapolitan song: 'Santa Lucia'

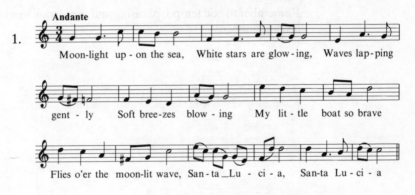

Traditional English song: 'Early one morning'

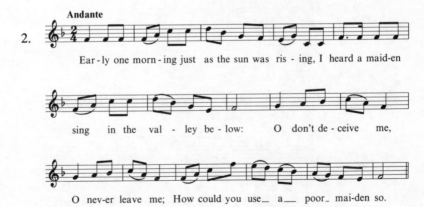

English carol: 'We've been awhile a-wandering'

Remember to add tempo, phrasing and expression marks to your
accompaniment.

CHAPTER FOUR

Chromatic harmony: secondary dominants

The word 'chromatic' means coloured. Throughout the history of music composers have looked for ways of making their music colourful. The ancient Greeks used a special chromatic scale pattern:

From the 16th century to the present day, many composers have used a mixture of diatonic and chromatic patterns in their music.

Diatonic notes form part of an ordinary scale, mode or key. *Chromatic* notes do not belong to that particular scale, mode or key and have accidentals which raise or lower the note. A *chromatic chord* has one or more notes 'foreign' to the key. *Chromatic harmony* uses a number of chromatic chords which are outside the key. *Chromatic melody notes* either (a) embellish the melody without changing the chord which accompanies them or (b) cause a change in the harmony as well as in the melody.

Mozart: Piano Concerto in A, K 488 (2nd movement)

(F♯ minor)

Secondary dominants

The falling 5th is the strongest root movement, and V–I is the strongest of all falling 5ths. The reason for this is the semitone between 7 and 8, the active leading note (7) pulling strongly to the tonic (8).

V of V (or a major triad on II)

By chromatically raising the 3rd of the minor triad on II, a changed note is produced which acts rather like a secondary leading note. A triad with this altered note becomes a secondary dominant (V of V) of the chord a 5th below.

C major: II V of V V I
G major: V I

Changing a chord into a secondary dominant makes the harmony both colourful and more active. V of V is the most important of all secondary dominants.

Traditional: 'Barbara Allen'

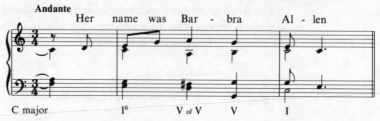

You already know that dominant chords are major and can be in root position, first and second inversion and that V[7] has four different notes so that three inversions are possible. Secondary dominants can be used in all these forms. V of V in C major can therefore be used in any of these positions.

V of V (a) and V[7] of V (b) in C major with inversions

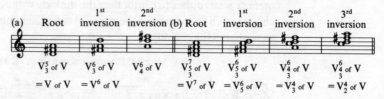

In this example, V[7] plays the part of a secondary dominant in its first inversion form.

Bach: *St John Passion*

V of II (or the major triad on VI)

The dominant of II has note 6 of a major scale as its root. The 3rd is raised to change the chord from minor to major, making it a secondary dominant.

In the following example, V of II is first heard in root position and then as a passing $^6_4$ chord.

Schumann: Novelette in F, Op. 21 no. 1

F major: V of II   II⁶   V$^6_4$ of II   II   V   I

*   = root position
+   = passing $^6_4$

V of III

The dominant of III has note 7 of the scale as its root. In a major scale chord VII is diminished, so two changes need to be made for the chord to become major and a secondary dominant: the 3rd and the 5th are both raised.

C major: I (III)   V of III   III   V⁷   I

Mendelssohn: Wedding March from *A Midsummer Night's Dream*

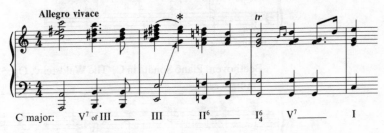

C major: V⁷ of III _____   III   II⁶ _____   I$^6_4$ V⁷ _____   I

*   = delayed resolution

V of III in a minor key occurs on the lowered seventh degree, and no changes need to be made since it is already major; often a minor 7th is added:

Bach: chorale *Aus tiefer Not schrei ich zu dir*

A minor: V   I   V⁷ of III   III⁶   VI   III   IV   V

V of IV

This is one of the most common of all secondary dominants. As V of IV is in fact the same as chord I in major keys, a lowered (minor) 7th is often added to make V^7 of IV. Adding the 7th in this way gives the chord its distinctive quality.

C major: { V of IV \ V^7 of IV   IV   V   I
        { I }

Schumann: At the Fireside from *Scenes of Childhood*, Op. 15 no. 8

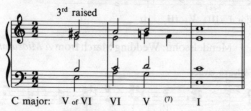

F major: I V^4_3 of IV IV V^7 I

V of VI

The dominant of VI has note 3 of a major scale as its root. As with the V of V and V of II, the 3rd of the chord is raised to make it major.

3rd raised

C major: V of VI   VI   V   (7)   I

Beethoven: Piano Sonata in C, 'The Waldstein', Op. 53 (1st movement)

Allegro con brio

p dolce   *cresc.*   *sf*

C major: VI V^7 of VI   IV V^4_3 I^6 II^6_5 I^6_4 V

V of VI in a minor key is diatonically a major chord.

       V of VI V^4_3 I

In the following example, V of VI is used first as a chromatic chord in G major, then as a diatonic chord in G minor.

Wagner: 'Star of Eve' from *Tannhäuser*

G major:I^6 II   G minor: V of VI   VI

Series of secondary dominants

Secondary dominants can follow one another in a pattern or sequence. You will find examples of these sequences in music of the 18th and 19th centuries. Notice the movement of the bass in this pattern. It is another example of the strong falling-5th root movement.

Bach: Prelude in F minor from *The Well-tempered Clavier*, Book 2

F minor: V^7 of IV   (IV) V^7 of III   (III)

In this example a sequence of secondary dominants is heard using the chord in its first inversion form (V_5^6), with the secondary leading notes rising to their octaves. The chords make rich, colourful and active harmony.

Beethoven: Piano Sonata in E flat, Op. 31 no. 3 (1st movement)

Bb major: I V_5^6 of VI   VI V_5^6 of IV   IV V_5^6 of II   II♮ V^6(of I)   I

V_5^6 I V_5^6 I

Preparing and resolving secondary dominants

Any chord may be used before a secondary dominant so long as the part-writing is smooth. To achieve this:

1. When a note (a) is chromatically altered (b), write both notes in the same part.

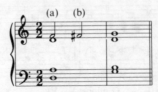

2. If the note which is to be altered is doubled in the previous chord, one of the parts moves chromatically (a), as in point **1**. The part with the doubled note (b) moves to a different note of the next chord.

Secondary dominants are often used and resolved like ordinary dominants:

1. They move by a falling 5th or a rising 4th (to their own tonic chord).
2. The altered leading note is not doubled.
3. The altered leading note moves up by step.

VI   V of V   V   I

As a general guide:

1. A note chromatically raised continues rising.
2. A note chromatically lowered continues falling.

Secondary dominants, like diatonic dominants, sometimes resolve in other ways. For example:

1. V of V can move to I_4^6 before moving to V.

C major: V of V I_4^6 V^7 I

2. A secondary dominant may move to another V^7.

C major: V^7 of II V^7 of V V^7 I

(See also the information on the secondary dominant series.)

Conclusion

1. Secondary dominants are chromatic chords which are foreign to the key you are in at the time.

2. They help to make harmony more active, rich and colourful.

3. Experiment by using some of these chords in your own writing but use them sparingly at first. The most useful are V of V, then V of II, V of IV and V of VI.

4. Try to find examples of secondary dominants and look to see how they are used.

5. Most importantly, always play or listen to the chords as they occur in music. You will then be able to identify them by ear as well as by eye.

WORK ON SECONDARY DOMINANTS

1. Rewrite these progressions raising the 3rd of each chord II to make a secondary dominant (V of V).

C major: II V^7 I   II   I$^6_4$ V^7 I   II VI^6 V$^6_5$ I   II   V^7 I

* = accented passing note

Play your answers. Transpose them into three different major keys (a) on paper, and (b) at the piano.

2. Prepare and resolve these secondary dominant chords.
Example:

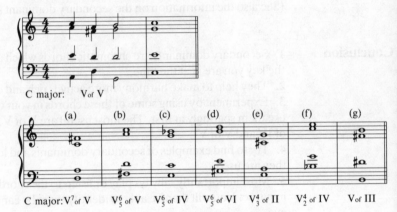

C major: V of V

C major: V^{7}of V   V$^6_5$ of V   V$^6_5$ of IV   V$^6_5$ of VI   V$^4_3$ of II   V$^4_2$ of IV   V of III

Transpose your answers into four different keys.

3. Write the following progressions for SATB (a) in D major, (b) in E flat major, (c) in F major, (d) in A major:
   (i) V of V, I$^6_4$, V^7, I   (ii) V^7 of II, V^7 of V, V^7, I

4. Write these progressions for SATB (a) in C minor, (b) in G minor, (c) in B Minor:
   (i) V$^6_5$ of IV, IV, V^7, I   (ii) V of III, III, V$^4_3$, I

5. Write this secondary dominant series for SATB (a) in C major, (b) in B flat major, (c) in G major:
   V^7 of III, V^7 of VI, V^7 of II, V^7 of V, V^7, I
The bass should follow the falling 5th pattern and the soprano should move downwards in semitones.

6. Using the chord pattern of the secondary dominant series in
G major from exercise **5**
a) add some chromatic embellishing notes to make a more
   interesting piece of music
b) compose a short piano piece in a style of your choice.

7. Analyse all chords, including the secondary dominants, in this
G major passage (the secondary dominants are either in root position
or in 1st inversion). Copy out the music and write the chord symbols
underneath the bass stave.

Beethoven: Piano Concerto No. 4, Op. 58 (1st movement)

G major

∗ = secondary dominants

8. Write an 8-bar progression for SATB in any key. Use two chords a
bar and include three different secondary dominants.

9. Harmonise these extracts and include some secondary dominant
chords.

Beethoven: Symphony No. 1 (1st movement)

C major

∗ = suggestions for secondary dominant chords
+ = chromatic melody notes

Spiritual: 'Standin' in de need of prayer'

G major

Beethoven: Piano Sonata in A flat, Op. 26 (1st movement)

3.

Compare your harmonisation with the originals.

10. Compose a short piece for piano (16 – 24 bars). Include the
following:
a) some secondary dominants in root position and different
inversions
b) chromatic embellishments (auxiliary and passing notes, scale and
arpeggio passages, turning patterns etc.).

Style in melody writing

The subject of melody writing covers many centuries and styles in the history of music. Study of the 20th century alone will reveal something of just how vast this subject really is.

First, there are different melodic styles in different countries. The music of India is based on ragas (something between a scale and a melody). There are hundreds of ragas and almost as many melodic styles in this one country alone. Compare Indian music with that of a European country such as Italy and the contrast is even more marked.

Second, there are many different kinds of music – folk, country, rock, pop, jazz, 'classical' – each with its own style or styles. In jazz alone there are gospel songs, spirituals, ragtime, swing, boogie-woogie, minstrel music, the blues and soul. Individual performers play a wide range of instruments and each has a distinctive style.

Third, there are many composers writing music in the 20th century, each using a particular way of shaping melody in their compositions.

This brief outline gives an idea of how wide the subject of melody really is. For the moment we shall have to limit our study to just a few important melodic styles.

Plainsong

Plainsong is the ancient melody of the church. This pure melody can still be heard today sung at some services, especially in Roman Catholic churches.

Sequence: *Victimae paschali laudes* ('Praises to the Paschal victim')

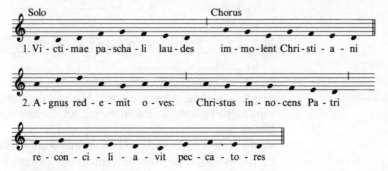

Plainsong:
1. Is a single line of vocal melody (monophonic).
2. Is usually unaccompanied.
3. Is in free rhythm – no time signature or regular bar-lines. The melody takes its rhythm from the natural accents of the words.
4. Is based on the church modes (See *Harmony, Melody and Composition*: Chapter 5).
5. Uses a medium range of notes.
6. Often has Latin words.

Word setting   There are four styles of word setting in plainsong:
                      1. Syllabic: one note of the melody to one syllable of the text.

Pa - ter no - ster qui es in cae - lis

2. Neumatic: a few (2–4) notes to each syllable.

Lux ae - - ter - - na

3. Psalmodic: several syllables to one repeated note.

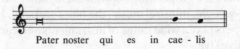

Pater noster qui es in cae - lis

4. Melismatic: many notes to one syllable.

Ky - ri - e_____ e - lei - son

There are more than 3000 plainsong melodies. The *Alleluia* is used for special church festivals.

Al-le-lu - ia (a)_____

(a) _____

Sing this *Alleluia*. After the word 'Alleluia' the rest of the melody is sung to the syllable 'a' (called the *jubilus* because of its joyful style). Notice that:
a) the style is melismatic – a flowing and wave-shape melody
b) it uses mainly stepwise movement but with some small leaps
c) it is in the Dorian mode
d) notes 1 or 5 of the mode, the most important, are used at the start and end of most sections
e) the phrases are not equal but are asymmetrical.

The 16th century and Palestrina

The 16th century was the golden age of unaccompanied vocal polyphony (polyphony is the sounding together of different strands of melody). Composers of this time paid careful attention to the melodic value of each voice. Motives move from voice to voice imitating one another. The style of polyphony:

1. Has melodic and rhythmic freedom in each vocal line.
2. Is generally calm and smooth.
3. The music is composed for between four and eight voices.
4. Melody is embellished with passing notes, auxiliary notes, suspensions and anticipations.
5. The modes are still used but there is a move towards major and minor tonality.
6. Composers started to introduce chromatic notes into their music.
7. Church composers were expected to avoid intervals difficult to sing.
8. Music was usually written without bar-lines.

Palestrina is one of the most important composers of the 16th century. His melody:

1. Is in a true vocal style – well written for the voice.
2. Moves mainly by step or small leaps.
3. Has free and smooth movement with a gentle flow.
4. The texture of the voice parts is light and clear.

Perhaps Palestrina's best known work is *Missa Papae Marcelli* ('Mass for Pope Marcellus') for six voices (SATTBB). The music is expressive, calm and beautiful. It begins with this motive:

Palestrina: Kyrie from *Missa Papae Marcelli*

Notice:
a) the flowing movement by step
b) the smooth, flowing melodic line, which starts with a repeated note heard three times but which has a general downward slope
c) the interval of a rising 4th – this appears at different times in other voices
d) the syncopation in bar 4
e) the F sharp chromatic note in bar 4.
   The *Sanctus* of the Mass has this tune which gradually unfolds.

Palestrina: Sanctus from *Missa Papae Marcelli*

There are more small leaps here (3rds as well as 4ths) but the general melodic style remains smooth and flowing.

Bach and Handel

A composer's style is difficult to describe for it depends on many things such as personality, background, training, experience and the way in which he uses melody, harmony, rhythm, form and instruments. This is particularly true of Bach and Handel. Both composers were born in Germany, and in the same year, but there were striking differences in their lives which influenced the kind of music each wrote. Bach is best known for his imaginative and clever harmony and counterpoint. We tend to forget that he had a great gift for melody writing. Bach's melodies are not in any one particular style. There are examples of melodies which have:

1. Precise and regular dance-like rhythms.

Bach: Minuet in G from *Anna Magdalena Klavierbüchlein*, no. 2

2. Flowing and decorated upward and downward patterns which outline the harmony.

Bach: Italian Concerto (2nd movement)

3. Exciting chromatic passages.

Bach: Prelude in A minor from *The Well-tempered Clavier*, Book 2

4. Dazzling and colourful rich passages.

Bach: 'And there were shepherds' from *Christmas Oratorio*

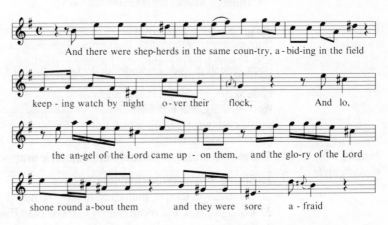

And there were shep-herds in the same coun-try, a-bid-ing in the field

keep-ing watch by night   o-ver their   flock,   And lo,

the an-gel of the Lord came up-on them,   and the glo-ry of the Lord

shone round a-bout them   and they were   sore   a-fraid

5. A simple motive expanded into a long and continuous melodic line (often using short, fast notes in different rhythmic patterns).

Bach: Gloria from *B minor Mass*

Glo   -   ri-a in   ex-cel   -   sis

Symbolism in Bach's melody

In his melodies, especially those set to words, Bach writes music to bring out the 'meaning' or mood of the words. Two examples of his musical symbolism are:

a) a downward chromatic note pattern for sadness

Bach: No. 16 from *B minor Mass*

b) continuous patterns of quavers or semi-quavers for joy.

Bach: Cantata no. 147

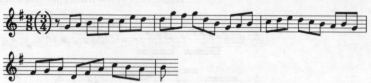

Bach also treats words like 'ascend', 'descend', 'quiet', and 'pain' with musical ideas which attempt to give the same kind of feeling.
For example:

Bach: chorale prelude *Durch Adams Fall ist ganz verderbt*
('Through Adam's fall mankind fell too')

Bach: chorale prelude *Erstanden ist der heilige Christ* ('Christ is arisen')

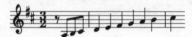

*Handel's
melodic style*

The main features of Handel's melodic style are:

1. Strong, often dotted rhythmic patterns.
2. Contrasts in tempo, melodic patterns, range.
3. Long phrases, but more clearly marked than Bach's.
4. Flowing melodies in a 'singing' (*cantabile*) style, often starting with a long held note.
5. Embellishments.
6. Accompanying harmony is more simple, direct and less chromatic than Bach's – I, V, and first inversion chords are common.
7. High tenor and bass parts, low soprano and alto in vocal music.

Handel: 'O Praise the Lord', Chandos Anthem no. 6

**Mozart and
Haydn**

There is a definite change in melodic style in the 18th century. The long and highly embellished melodies of earlier composers give way to a more simple, clear and compact style of melody. Phrases are shorter and often symmetrical.

Haydn and Mozart both influenced each other, but there are a few interesting differences in their melodic styles. Both composers believed that melody should be based on the voice. Haydn wrote: 'If you want to know whether you have written anything worthwhile, sing it to yourself without accompaniment'. Haydn's themes are often strong, cheerful and lively in a folk-like style.

Haydn: Symphony No. 94, 'The Surprise' (2nd movement)

Mozart favours a singing, *cantabile* style. Shaped on the human voice, his melodies are more fine and delicate.

Mozart: 'Là ci darem la mano' from *Don Giovanni*

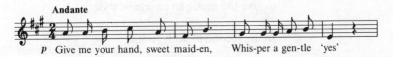

Mozart makes greater use of embellishments, and his harmony and melody are more chromatic than Haydn's simple and diatonic style. Haydn's phrases are generally clear-cut and regular. Mozart's can be more extended and irregular.

Mozart: Symphony No. 40, K 550 (3rd movement)

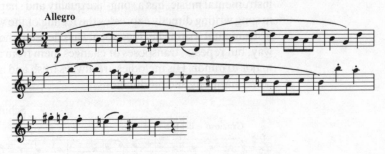

Play these two contrasting melodies from Mozart's 40th Symphony:

Mozart: Symphony No. 40, K 550 (1st movement)

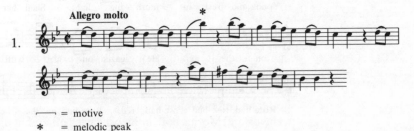

⎯⎯ = motive
* = melodic peak

Mozart: Symphony No. 40, K 550 (1st movement)

Notice in the first melody:

1. The melody grows out of a three-note motive.
2. Phrases are symmetrical, each evenly balanced.
3. The overall curve is an arch-shaped melody.
4. The step-wise movement, the leap of a 6th to the melodic peak, followed by more step-wise movement.
5. The harmony of bars 1–4 is a broken chord of G minor – this helps to give the music an energetic style.

In the second melody, notice:

1. The calm, chromatic movement which contrasts with the urgent movement of the first tune.
2. The melodic shape – two downward slopes.
3. The rhythmic contrasts.

Schubert

Schubert composed over 600 songs. His melodic style, even in instrumental music, has a song-like quality and shape. Schubert's style in song writing directly expresses the feeling of the words. In instrumental writing he does not always develop themes in a detailed way, but repeats, transposes or changes them from minor to major or major to minor. His melodies are always fresh and natural, full of clever harmony and modulations.

Schubert: *Heidenröslein*

Play or sing this melody. Notice that:

1. The mood of the song is described by the words above the music – *grazioso* (Italian for 'gracefully') and *lieblich* (German for 'friendly').
2. The 7-line poem is asymmetrical. Schubert writes answering 2-bar phrases for lines 1 and 2, and a 6-bar phrase for lines 3, 4 and 5. The phrase for lines 6 and 7 slowly rises up the scale with a pause at the climax on high G. He returns to the original tempo for the ending.
3. Medium range of the melody is just 8 notes.
4. Movement is mainly by step.
5. All phrases are developed from the opening motive (bars 1–2).
6. The melodic style is simple, direct and flowing.

Tchaikovsky   Tchaikovsky had a gift for melody and exciting rhythm. His melodic style:

1. Repeats and transposes rather than develops ideas. Flowing and emotional melody is not as easy to develop as short, rhythmical motives.
2. Often uses a pause within a phrase.
3. Often has a showy climax near the end, especially in his songs.
4. Is full of emotion and feeling.
5. Has spectacular climaxes.
6. Has sweeping up and down runs.
7. Has rich harmonies.
8. Is typically Russian – full of contrasts: sometimes sad, sometimes happy, rich and impulsive.

In the Overture-fantasy *Romeo and Juliet,* Tchaikovsky uses three ideas from Shakespeare's play. The first melody is like a Russian hymn and represents Friar Lawrence:

Tchaikovsky: Overture-fantasy *Romeo and Juliet*

The second melody is about the hostility between the two families of Verona:

Tchaikovsky: Overture-fantasy *Romeo and Juliet*

The third melody concerns the lovers, Romeo and Juliet:

Tchaikovsky: Overture-fantasy *Romeo and Juliet*

Notice the sharp contrasts between the second and third melody. These are typical of Tchaikovsky's music in general. Theme 2 is powerful and fiery with syncopated rhythm. Theme 3 is a long melody, full of warmth and kindness. Notice in theme 3:

a) the melodic wave-shapes
b) the rich chromatic movement (rich harmony and scoring for instruments is not seen here)
c) the falling intervals
d) the use of sequence

WORK ON STYLE IN MELODY WRITING

Analyse the following melodies by writing a summary of the main features and style of each. It may help you in your task to collect some information along these lines.

1. Research by reading something about the historical background of the period and/or composer.

2. Play and sing the melody several times.

3. Write down details of the FORM – for example, number of bars, phrases, phrase lengths (symmetrical/asymmetrical).

4. Note details of MELODIC and RHYTHMIC PATTERNS – for example, movement by step and/or leap, range, melodic shape(s), motives, ways of treating motives (sequence, inversion, etc.), climaxes, key, scales/modes, chromatic embellishments.

5. You will gradually begin to build up a picture from this information about the general style of the melody – for example, is the melody smooth, spiky, flowing, decorated, simple, symmetrical? (Chapter 13 in *Harmony, Melody and Composition* gives a more detailed step-by-step plan for music analysis.)

Alleluia: *Vidimus stellam*

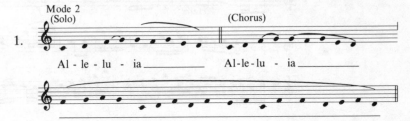

Palestrina: madrigal 'Ahi, che quest' occhi miei'

Translation: 'Ah, that these my eyes, which once were glad, should have become fountains of sadness, which pour out tears by day and night.'

Bach: Badinerie from Orchestral Suite no. 2

3.

Mozart: Divertimento no. 17, K 334

4.

Schumann: Symphony No. 1 (2nd movement)

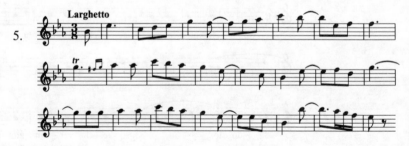

5.

Tchaikovsky; Symphony No. 5 (2nd movement)

CHAPTER FIVE

Modulation to the dominant

Modulation is a change from one key to another. Chromatic notes or chords (such as secondary dominants) briefly colour the music, then are cancelled. When an accidental (or chromatic note) makes a modulation it is used for a longer time so that a cadence can establish the new key.

From the 16th century to the present day, modulation has been used for:

1. Variety and contrast, especially in longer pieces.
2. Change of mood.
3. Colour.
4. Increasing harmonic motion.
5. To stress different parts or sections of a piece.

Modulation from I to V

Just as I–V is the most basic and closely related movement in melody and harmony, so the most important modulation is from the tonic to the dominant key.

Stages in modulation

There are usually four stages in a modulation:

1. Establish the home key	2. Pivot chord	3. Enter the new key	4. Establish the new key

Stage 1. Establish the home key – the tonic. Before a modulation takes place the home key must be made clear. This can be done by using:
a) a series of chords which includes a cadence
b) primary chords.

Stage 2. Pivot chord. A pivot chord is one which belongs to both keys – the tonic and the new key. Pivot chords join or link the two keys smoothly together. There are four pivot chords shared by any tonic and its dominant key.
For example:

C major: I   III   V   VI
G major: IV   VI   I   II

You should choose a pivot chord which moves strongly to V of the new key. II or IV are usually best when modulating to the dominant.

Stage 3. Enter the new key. You can enter the new key:

a) in melody – by a modulating note (that is, a note belonging to the new key but not to the old). The note will have an accidental and is usually note 7 (the leading note). In the modulation from C to G major, for example, the keys are closely related. The only note which does not occur in both keys is F sharp (note 7 of G). Use this note to enter G after the pivot chord.

b) in harmony – by a modulating chord (that is, one belonging to the new key but not to the old). The modulating chord is usually V, V^7 or VII^6.

Stage 4. Establish the new key. In a true modulation, a cadence (usually perfect) is needed to establish the new key in the mind of the listener. If there is no cadence after stage 3, the changed chord could be heard simply as a secondary dominant chromatic chord.

Let us look at the four stages of a modulation in a piece of music.

Schütz: *The Christmas Story*

Stage 1. Home key (F major) is established through the use of primary chords (I. IV, V).

Stage 2. Pivot chord (VI in F major; II in C major).

Stage 3. V of C major, with a B natural foreign to F major.

Stage 4. New key (C major) is established with a perfect cadence.

Inversions of V, V^7 and VII as modulating chords

Use inversions of these chords to modulate when smoother, more gentle movement to the new key is required. For example:

Beethoven: Piano Sonata in E, Op. 109 (3rd movement)

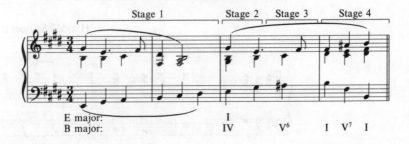

There are three kinds of modulation.

1. Abrupt modulation. The music plunges into the new key without using a pivot chord as a link.

Haydn: Symphony No. 104, 'The London' (2nd movement)

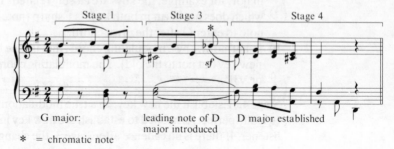

G major: leading note of D   D major established
                            major introduced

* = chromatic note

Note: part-writing in abrupt modulations:

a) When a diatonic note changes chromatically into a modulating note, both notes move smoothly in the same part. The chord is different for each note.

b) The new leading note (7) moves to its new tonic.

c) The new leading note is not doubled.

2. Quick modulation. The four stages take place quickly, and stages 3 and 4 become one.

Bach: chorale *Ach Gott und Herr*

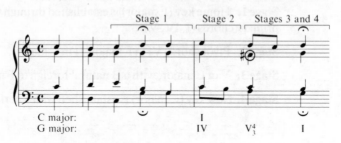

C major:
G major: I
                                      IV   V$^4_3$ I

3. Gradual modulation. In a true modulation, musical 'time' is an important factor. The four stages take more time so that the listener becomes gradually tuned-in to the new key.

Handel: Minuet from *Water Music*

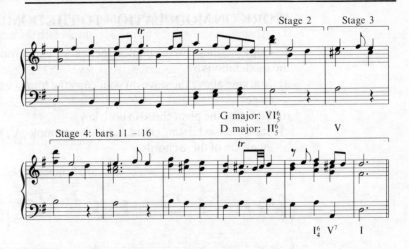

In the first section of this movement, stage 1 takes 8 bars to establish the home key (G major). The pivot chord (stage 2) lasts for one complete bar. The modulating chord (V) is heard for one full bar as the music enters the new key (stage 3). There follow a further 6 bars before a perfect cadence is heard in the new key (D major).

Return to the home key (V to I)

To return to the home key the stages work the other way around.

Stage 1. The dominant key has already been established.
Stage 2. Pivot chord (not in abrupt modulations).
Stage 3. Enter the home key by introducing a modulating note or chord which occurs only in the tonic.
Stage 4. Set up a perfect cadence to re-establish the home key.

Hymn Edinburgh 1635: *London New*

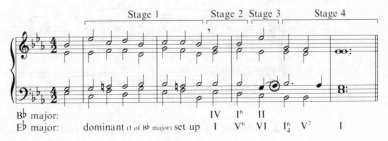

WORK ON MODULATION TO THE DOMINANT

1. Copy out these two examples, then play them through. Analyse the modulations by

a) Marking above the stave on your copy the four stages. Name each stage.

b) Describe the pivot chord in both keys.

c) State the modulating chord used – for example, V, V⁷, VII or an inversion of these chords.

Mozart: Symphony No. 25, K 183 (Trio)

Bach: Brandenburg Concerto No. 1

2. Analyse the various stages in these modulations and say whether they are abrupt, quick or gradual.

Traditional Welsh melody: 'All through the night'

Bach: chorale *Gottes Sohn ist kommen*

Luther (attrib.): chorale *Ein' feste Burg*

3. Where does (a) the secondary dominant and (b) the modulation occur in this extract? Give the bar numbers for each and reasons for your choice.

Traditional Scottish melody: 'The Blue Bells of Scotland'

4. Write four different sets of chord progressions of 8–12 bars modulating from these tonic keys to their dominants:
   (a) A major   (c) B flat major
   (b) E major   (d) D flat major
Mark in the stages.

5. Write two abrupt modulations (SATB) from (a) G major to its dominant and (b) E flat major to its dominant.

6. Write two quick modulations (SATB) from (a) D major to its dominant and (b) F major to its dominant.

7. Transpose each of your answers to questions, 4, 5 and 6 at the piano into four different major keys.

8. Compose a piece for piano (about 16 bars) in a style of your choice, but include a gradual modulation to the dominant *and* a return to the tonic key.

9. Harmonise these two melodies (which include a modulation to the dominant) in the style of the given openings.

Ford: madrigal 'Since first I saw your face'

Handel: Courante in F

Phrase symmetry and balance

When one phrase exactly equals another in length (for example, 4 bars and 4 bars) it is called symmetrical.

Music and dance have always been closely linked and symmetrical music probably began as a result of dance patterns. Regular patterns of dance steps would need regular patterns of music. This in turn led to repeated motives and phrases in music.

Parallel phrases

Parallel phrases are a more developed design which has been used for centuries by composers. The parallel phrase consists of two phrases which are alike in length and material, but different in their cadences. This design gives music symmetry and balance but also some contrast.

Lynes: Sonatina in C, Op. 39 no. 1

Parallel phrases vary in length from 4 to 16 bars. They are either:

1. Independent – that is, complete pieces; or
2. Dependent – part of a longer composition.

Independent parallel phrases

The halfway cadence is usually imperfect, but can end on IV, V of V or another secondary dominant. The second phrase usually starts in a similar way to the first, but the opening can be changed in small ways for variety. This is done by using:

1. A sequence.

Mozart: Sonata in C, K 6/3 (Menuetto I)

2. Embellishments.

Field: Nocturne no. 6 in F

3. Inversion.

Wagner: Elizabeth's Prayer from *Tannhäuser*

4. Extension. **5.** Simplifying. **6.** Expansion. **7.** Interval change. **8.** Pitch change. (See *Harmony, Melody and Composition*: Chapters 8 and 9.)

Parallel phrases may be balanced and symmetrical, but details within the phrase may also be different.

Spiritual: 'Liza Jane'

The two phrases can sound rather separated or self-contained. To avoid this feeling composers use three different methods to keep the music flowing.

1. The melody continues over the midway cadence point.

Mozart: Piano Sonata in B flat, K 570 (3rd movement)

2. The melody stops at the cadence but other parts continue moving.

Himmel: *Mignon*

3. Melody and accompaniment flow through the cadence.

Beethoven: Piano Sonata in G, Op. 79 (1st movement)

Notice: (a) the sequence; (b) the pitch change; (c) the continuing harmony and melody.

WORK ON PHRASE SYMMETRY AND BALANCE

1. Analyse the following symmetrical, parallel phrases in this way:

a) copy and play the phrases

b) mark in the two phrases and cadences

c) say how the second phrase is varied – sequence, embellishments, inversion, or another method(s)

d) does the melody or accompaniment continue through the midway cadence?

Beethoven: Sonatina in F, Wo050 (Rondo)

Mozart: 'Non più andrai, from *The Marriage of Figaro*

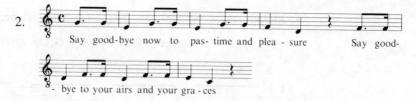

Mozart: *An Chloe*

Schubert: Scherzo in B flat, D 593 no. 1

* = chromatic notes

2. Compose two parallel phrases in any key. Indicate the harmony at the cadence points.

3. Compose these different types of parallel phrases:
a) the second phrase starts as a sequence of the first (E flat major)
b) the second phrase is an embellished version of the first (E major)
c) the second phrase is an approximate inversion of the first
   (G minor)
Sketch in the cadences.

4. Compose parallel phrases in a style suitable for the piano. The melody should continue moving through the midway cadence.

5. Compose parallel phrases for voice with piano accompaniment. The vocal line rests at the midway point but movement continues in the accompaniment.

Write on three staves. You may use these words or make up your own.

> O mighty-mouthed inventor of harmonies,
> O skilled to sing of Time or Eternity.
> (Tennyson)

CHAPTER SIX

Modulation to other closely related keys

Modulation is not an important part of all kinds of music. It does not appear, for example, in:

1. Music composed before about 1600. This was based on the church modes and had no major or minor key systems as we know them.
2. The music of India and China.
3. Some music of the 20th century. Certain composers have used different systems such as atonality. Atonal music is not in a key: there are no key centres, tonic notes or related chords.

But modulation is an important ingredient of Western music composed after about 1600 and of much of the popular music today.

Modulation from I to VI

In the years following the introduction of our major and minor key system, modulation was generally to closely related keys. A closely related key is one with a key signature the same as the tonic, or just one sharp or flat more or less than the tonic key. There are five keys closely related to any tonic major key. In C major, for example, the closely related keys are:

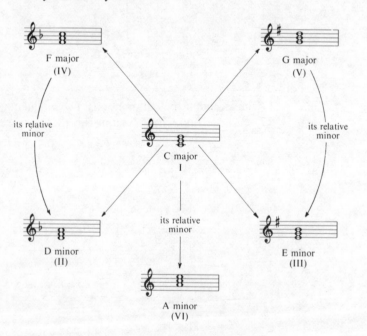

You have looked at modulation to the dominant, the most common key change, in Chapter 5. The next most closely related key is VI (the Relative Minor).

Modulation	Example	Pivot chords		Modulating notes (in new key)	Modulating chords	Common cadence patterns in new key
I	C major	I II IV VI VII				I_4^6 - $V^{(7)}$ - I
to	to					II - $V^{(7)}$ - I
VI	A minor	LIII IV VI I II		R6 7	RIV V	IV - $V^{(7)}$ - I

These two keys, each with the same key signature, have many chords in common. You will remember the three versions of minor scales:

1. Harmonic minor – has a raised 7 (R7) which appears in the modulating chords V, V^7 and VII.

R7 = raised 7

American Civil War song: 'John Brown's Body'

C major: VI
A minor: I   V   I   * = modulating note

2. The ascending melodic minor has two modulating notes – R6 and R7 – each with its own modulating chords. For example:

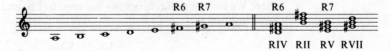

Notice the common patterns here:

Bach: chorale *Herr Christ der ein'ge Gottessohn*

A major: VI
F# minor: I RIV_5^6 - V_5^6 II_5^6 V   I

Raised notes 6 and 7 use raised chords IV^6 and V^6 (or VII), or IV_5^6 and V_5^6 as in the example.

3. The descending melodic minor of VI has all the same notes and chords as its relative major key (I).

As the two keys I and VI have many chords in common, it is quite easy to write a quick modulation by using V (or IV and V) at almost any point in a phrase. A definite pivot chord is not really necessary.

Handel: Aria from *Water Music*

G major: V   I   II⁶   VII⁶₅   VI   VI⁶₄

E minor: LVII   LIII   IV⁶   II⁶₅   I   I⁶₄   V   I

L = lowered

Modulation from I to II

Modulation	Example	Pivot chords	Modulating notes (in new key)	Modulating chords	Common cadence patterns in new key
I to II	C major to D minor	I II IV V LVII I LIII RIV	L6 7	LIV V	IV - V - I II⁽⁶⁾ - V⁽⁷⁾ - I

In this modulation, to II (the relative minor of the subdominant), there are two modulating notes – lowered 6 (L6) and raised 7 (R7; the most important).

There are four pivot chords. For example:

C major: I   II   IV   V

D minor: LVII   I   LIII   RIV

Ravenscroft: hymn-tune *Bristol*

G major: II
A minor: I

* = modulating notes

In this example the modulating note (7) appears in the tenor, followed by L6 in the bass. R7 and L6 are often heard close together in this modulation.

Notice here that:

1. L6 comes before R7 (modulating notes).
2. Chord II⁶ comes before V⁷ (modulating chords).

Dvořák: *Te Deum*

Moderato

G major:
A minor: I   II⁶   V⁷   I

Modulation from I to III

Modulation	Example	Pivot chords	Modulating notes (in new key)	Modulating chords	Common cadence patterns in new key
I to III	C major to E minor				$V^{(7)}$ - I II^6 - V - I II^6_5 - I^6_4 - $V^{(7)}$ - I

Brahms: Waltz in A flat, Op. 39 no. 15

Ab major:	I⁶		VI	I	VI	I	III⁶		
	I^6		VI	I	VI	I	III^6		
C minor:	VI⁶	IV		VI	IV	VI	I⁶	V⁷	I

Notice in the above quick modulation, to III (the relative minor of the dominant), that:

1. Stages 3 and 4 are combined (the modulating notes immediately become the cadence in the new key).

2. The modulating chord (V) includes both modulating notes (7 and 2). They are often heard sounding together.

3. The modulation has a stronger drive than I to II.

4. All of the three common pivot chords are heard before the modulation takes place. Thought of another way, chords of the tonic key lead straight into the new V.

Modulation from I to IV

Modulation	Example	Pivot chords				Modulating notes (in new key)	Modulating chords			Common cadence patterns in new key
I	C major	I	II	IV	VI					V^7 - I
to	to									IV - I - V - I
IV	F major	V	VI	I	III	4	II	IV	V^7	II^6 - V - I

Bach: Two-part Invention no. 14

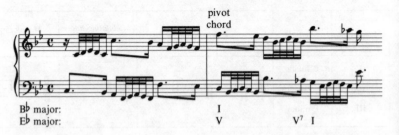

		pivot chord		
Bb major:		I		
Eb major:		V	V⁷	I

Notice that:

1. Modulating from I to IV often occurs towards the end of a piece. The subdominant is a darker, more gentle key than the dominant.

2. Other related keys have 7 as a modulating note – the subdominant has lowered 4 (L4).

3. There is no new chord V in the new key. V^7 can, however, be used to introduce the modulating note (L4).

WORK ON MODULATION TO OTHER CLOSELY RELATED KEYS

1. Write (a) the pivot chords, (b) modulating note(s) and
(c) modulating chords for these modulations:
(i) D major to G major   (iii) B flat major to D minor
(ii) E major to F sharp minor   (iv) A flat major to F minor

2. Write four different progressions of six chords each (SATB) to
illustrate these modulations:
(i) F major to D minor   (iii) A major to C sharp minor
(ii) G major to A minor   (iv) E flat major to A flat major
Write chords 1 and 2 in the tonic key; 3 as a pivot chord; 4 as a
modulating chord; 5 and 6 as a cadence in the new key. Identify and
label each stage of the modulation. Play each of these progressions
transposed into a different key.

3. Analyse these musical extracts by marking in:
a) The four stages of modulation
b) The modulating notes and chords
c) The chord symbols.

Bach: Minuet from French Suite no. 3

D major

Kirchhoff: Bourfee

F major

Heller: Study in C, Op. 45 no. 1

3.

C major

4. Harmonise these melodies in a suitable style; each includes at least one modulation to a closely related key.

Traditional Irish melody: 'The Minstrel Boy'

1.

D major

Handel: Air in B flat

2.

B♭ major

5. Compose a piece for piano (16–24 bars) modulating to three closely related keys, then back to the tonic.

Contrasting phrases

In two contrasting phrases the melody and cadences change but the phrases balance in length and general style. When writing contrasting phrases it is important to have some kind of unity as well as contrast. Here are some ideas for you to hear and try which will help bind together the contrasting phrases.

1. Repeated rhythm.

Traditional Irish melody: 'Hot Asphalt'

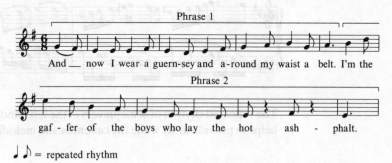

And __ now I wear a guern-sey and a-round my waist a belt. I'm the

gaf - fer of the boys who lay the hot ash - phalt.

♩ ♪ = repeated rhythm

The two phrases of this folk song are contrasting, but the constant crotchet-quaver rhythm helps to keep a sense of unity.

2. Melodic shape.

Musorgsky: Bydło from *Pictures from an Exhibition*

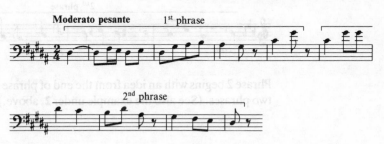

A broad, general arch-shape helps to bind these two phrases together.

3. Repeated patterns in the accompaniment.

Mozart: Piano Sonata in F, K 332 (2nd movement)

The repeated rhythm of semiquavers in the left hand accompaniment helps to provide unity while the cadences and melodic ideas contrast.

4. Recurring melodic fragments.

Beethoven: Piano Sonata in E flat, Op. 31 no. 3 (Menuetto)

Phrase 2 begins with an idea from the end of phrase 1, thus linking the two phrases. (See also the example under **2**, above.)

WORK ON CONTRASTING PHRASES

1. Play through these contrasting phrases. Then say which one of the four ideas mentioned in the chapter is used to help unify the phrases.

Beethoven: Piano Sonata in A flat, Op. 26 (1st movement)

1.

Reger: *Über Stock und Stein*, Op. 17 no. 5

2.

Beethoven: Piano Sonata in A flat, Op. 110 (3rd movement)

3.

Mozart: Piano Concerto in D, K 537 (1st movement)

2. Compose contrasting phrases (of the same number of bars each) to illustrate unity through:
a) repeated rhythm
b) repeated accompaniment patterns
c) melodic shape
d) a similar melodic fragment used at the start of each phrase.

Write in a different key and time signature for each set of phrases. Remember to contrast the melody and cadences.

CHAPTER SEVEN

Modulation from the minor to closely related keys

A minor key centre has five closely related keys. You will remember that a closely related key has the same key signature as the tonic or just one sharp or flat more or less than the tonic. In A minor, for example, the closely related keys are:

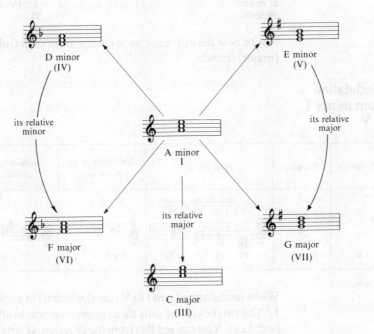

Modulation from I to III (the relative major) and from I to V are the two most often heard in traditional music.

Modulation from minor I to III

Modulation	Example	Pivot chords	Modulating notes (in new key)	Modulating chords	Common cadence patterns in new key
I to III	A minor to C major	I II LIII IV VI LVII VI VII I II IV V	5	V	$V^{(7)}$ - I IV - $V^{(7)}$ - I $II^{(6)}$ - V - I $IV(^6_5)$ - V - I

Nearly all the triads of a minor key occur in its relative major key, so there is a wide choice of pivot chords. When the tonic minor has been set-up or established, all that is often needed for the modulation to III (the relative major) is a simple cadence.

Bach: chorale *Nicht so traurig*

G minor: I^6 I   IV LIII^6
B♭ major: VI^6 VI II I^6 V - I

Notice how the music seems to change from dark (minor) to brighter (major) sounds.

Modulation from minor I to V

Modulation	Example	Pivot chords		Modulating notes (in new key)	Modulating chords	Common cadence patterns in new key
I	A minor		melodic descending			IV - V
to	to	I	LIII LV LVII			IV - I
V	E minor	IV VI I LIII		R6 7 2	II V	IV - $V^{(7)}$ - I

When modulating from I to V (the dominant) in minor keys:

1. The two keys have only three notes common to all scale forms of both keys. You can see this from the diagram. (Certain other notes are common to keys I and V, but only in certain forms of each scale).

A minor (harmonic) ascending

A minor (melodic) ascending

A minor (melodic) descending

E minor (harmonic) ascending

E minor (melodic) ascending

E minor (melodic) descending

2. V can be entered by using notes 2 or 7, but both notes need to be changed in the modulating chord V.

3. There are few pivot chords. Only one chord – I in the tonic key, IV in the dominant key – is common to all forms of both keys.

Gedike: *Petite pièce*, Op. 6 no. 2

The following passage shows a modulation from F minor to C minor using III (descending F melodic minor) /VI (C minor) as a pivot chord. It moves straight to V of the new key.

Beethoven: *Egmont Overture*

Modulation from minor I to VII

Modulation	Example	Pivot chords				Modulating notes *(in new key)*	Modulating chords	Common cadence patterns in new key
I	A minor	I	LIII	LV	LVII			$V^{(7)}$ - I
								V^6 - I
to	to							I_4^6 - V - I
VII	G major	II	IV	VI	I	7	V	IV - VII^6 - I

In the modulation from minor I to VII (relative major of V):

1. The two keys have very similar scales:

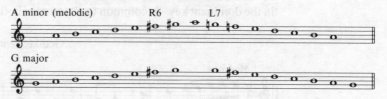

2. To change key, notes of the melodic scale are used – 6 is raised and 7 is lowered.

3. Chord I of the home key (II of the new key) is the most common pivot chord.

Bach: chorale *Da Jesus an dem Kreuze stund*

A minor: IV⁶   V   I
G major: II   I⁶   VI   IV   VII⁶   I

This is a quick modulation, as stages 3 and 4 are combined.

Modulation from minor I to IV

Modulation	Example	Pivot chords	Modulating notes (in new key)	Modulating chords	Common cadence patterns in new key
I	A minor	IV VI			V - I⁽⁶⁾ - IV - I
to	to				II⁶₅ - V - I
					IV - V - I
IV	D minor	I LIII	♭6 7	II IV VI V	V - IV - V - I

Both keys in the modulation from minor I to IV (the subdominant) have a dark quality. The modulation is often heard towards the end of a piece. Notice that:

1. Both modulating notes (L6 and R7) are generally used.

2. The key may change without the use of a pivot chord. The method is quite simple: the 3rd of chord I (home key) rises by a semitone to introduce the R7 of the new key. Chord I then becomes chord V of the new key.

Bach: Trio from French Suite no. 3

B minor: I
E minor: V⁷   I⁶₄   V⁷ _____ I   IV   V   I

⟶ = semitone rise to R7 of the new key

In this extract, the music seems to jump straight into the new key by
using chord I of the old key with a raised 3rd ('tierce de Picardie').
This chord immediately becomes V of the new key.

Handel: Aria from *Water Music*

G minor: I   V   I
C minor: V   I⁶ IV⁷ V   I

Modulation from minor I to VI

Modulation	Example	Pivot chords	Modulating notes (in new key)	Modulating chords	Common cadence patterns in new key
I to VI	A minor to F major	I LIII IV VI / III V VI I	♭o / 4	II IV V⁷	II⁶ - V⁽⁷⁾ - I / II - V⁽⁷⁾ - I

The modulation from minor I to VI (the relative major of IV) is heard
mainly in longer compositions.

Chopin: Prelude in C minor, Op. 28 no. 20

Largo

ff

C minor: I   VI ♭ ♭
A♭ major: III   I   IV   V⁷   I

WORK ON MODULATIONS FROM THE MINOR TO CLOSELY RELATED KEYS

1. Write (a) the pivot chords, (b) modulating note(s) and (c) modulating chords for these modulations:

  (i) D minor to G minor   (iv) C minor to B flat major

  (ii) E minor to G major   (v) G minor to E flat major

  (iii) F sharp minor to C sharp minor

2. Write five different progressions of six chords each (SATB) to illustrate these modulations:

  (i) F minor to C minor   (iv) B flat minor to E flat minor

  (ii) B minor to D major   (v) D minor to B flat major

  (iii) C sharp minor to B major

Write chords 1 and 2 in the tonic key; 3 as a pivot chord; 4 as a modulating chord; 5 and 6 as a cadence in the new key. Identify and label each stage of the modulation. Play each of these progressions transposed into three different keys.

3. Analyse these musical extracts by marking in:

a) the four stages of modulation (three stages if a quick or abrupt modulation)

b) the modulating notes and chords

c) the chord symbols

Bach: chorale *Herr Gott, nun schleuss den Himmel auf*

Bach: Echo from Partita in B minor

Damon's Psalter 1579: hymn *Southwell*

Lord   Je - sus think on   me,   And   purge a - way my   sin;

Mozart: Piano Sonata in A minor, K 310 (1st movement)

Bach: Prelude in D minor from *The Well-tempered Clavier*, Book 2

4. Harmonise these melodies in a suitable style; each includes at least one modulation to a closely related key.

Sohren: *Gute Bäume bringen*

Handel: song 'Sans y penser'

2.

E minor   G major

E minor   D major   G major

A minor   E minor

5. Compose a piece for piano (16–24 bars) modulating to three closely related keys, then back to the tonic. Start your piece in B minor or G minor.

Asymmetrical phrases

Melodic phrases can be clearly marked, balanced and equal in length (symmetrical). But throughout musical history, composers have also been interested in writing melodies which are less regular, less balanced and less rigid.

Plainsong, as you have seen, is often in a free, flowing style. 20th-century composers have used unorthodox time signatures (for example, $\frac{5}{8}$, $\frac{7}{8}$,$\frac{9}{16}$) to achieve irregular groupings of notes and irregular phrases. Some composers have stopped using time signatures and bar-lines altogether so that their melody, like plainsong, may be flexible and asymmetrical.

Asymmetrical phrases can occur:

1. As two free-flowing phrases of different lengths. Even though the phrases are irregular they seem to go well together:

Schumann: Piano Sonata 'für die Jugend', Op. 118 no. 1

2. When the second of two balanced phrases is lengthened (extension):

Handel: Bourrée from *Fireworks Music*

Copland: Suite from *Billy the Kid*

3. When the second of two balanced phrases is expanded in the middle rather than at the end of the phrase (expansion):

Reger: *Versöhnung* ('Reconciliation'), Op. 17 no. 20

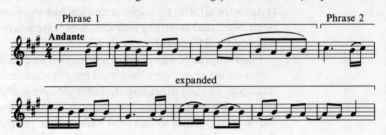

WORK ON ASYMMETRICAL PHRASES

1. Analyse these asymmetrical phrases by saying why each is irregular.

Stravinsky: Gavotte from *Pulcinella*

Folk song: 'Through bushes and through briars'

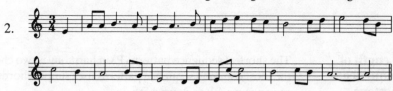

Mozart: Clarinet Quintet, K 581 (2nd movement)

Bizet: Entr'acte Intermezzo from *Carmen*

2. Compose three melodies consisting of asymmetrical phrases:

a) for oboe (A major), where the phrases are simply of different lengths

b) for bass voice (G minor), where the second phrase is longer than the first by extension

c) for violin (C major), where the second phrase is expanded.

3. Harmonise your melodies from exercise **2** in a suitable style for a piano accompaniment.

CHAPTER EIGHT

Sequences in harmony

A sequence (S) is the repetition of a melodic or harmonic pattern at a higher or lower level of pitch. Melodic sequences occur in one voice. Harmonic sequences occur in all voices. (For melodic sequences, see *Harmony, Melody and Composition*: Chapter 8.)

Sequences can help to:

1. Provide both variety and unity.
2. Build up a short idea into a longer phrase.
3. Add strong movement and drive to music.
4. Build up the drama to a climax (rising sequences).

Length of sequence pattern

The shortest sequence pattern (P) in harmony is two chords. One of the most common sequence patterns uses simple chords with roots moving up a 4th or down a 5th.

I IV II V III VI

P = Pattern
S = Sequence

Mozart: Sonata for Two Pianos, K 448 (2nd movement)

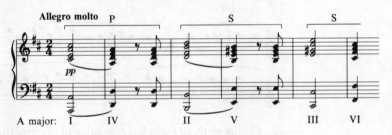

A major: I IV II V III VI

A sequence pattern can be as long as a complete phrase.

Loeillet: Gigue from Suite in G minor

There are examples of sequence patterns which are more than 20 bars long, but these are used in longer compositions and are more difficult to recognize.

Number of sequences

The usual number of sequences after the first pattern is one, two or three. After the third sequence composers usually change the pattern or give it up. There are exceptions to this. Music in the time of Bach and Handel sometimes has more than three repetitions of the pattern.

Bach: Organ Fugue in D, BWV 532

Types of harmonic sequence

Harmonic sequences can be:

1. Exact (real sequences) – all ingredients of the pattern (melody, chord, rhythm and intervals) are the same in each of the sequences; in effect, the music has been exactly transposed to another key.

Mozart: Piano Sonata in G, K 283

E minor: V   I   V   I   D minor: V   I   V   I

ES = Exact sequence

2. Varied (tonal sequences) – the repetition is made without leaving the original key, so that some of the intervals come out larger or smaller, generally by a semitone.

Wagner: *Die Meistersinger von Nürnberg*

C major: V _____ (I)

VS = Varied sequence   ✳ = diminished chord   + = minor chord   ⧺ = major chord

3. Modal – the repetition is made in a new key, but the new key is minor to the pattern's major, or major to the pattern's minor.

Mozart: Symphony No. 29, K 201 (1st movement)

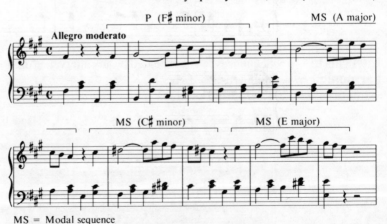

MS = Modal sequence

4. Free – the pattern is used in a loose or free way. The original pattern is easily identifiable but several ingredients may change.

Beethoven: Piano Sonata in C sharp minor, 'The Moonlight', Op. 27 no. 2
(3rd movement)

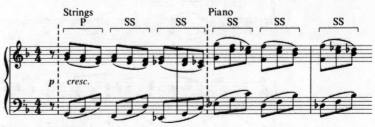

FS = Free
sequence

5. Syncopated – the accentuation of the pattern is disturbed. In the following example the pattern is of one-and-a-half beats' duration while the time signature is four beats to a bar. The result is that on each repetition a different part of the pattern occurs on the regular beats of the bar; in other words, the result is cross-accentuation.

Brahms: Piano Quintet, Op. 34 (1st movement)

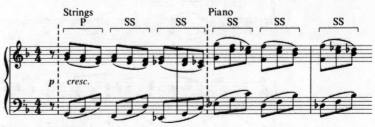

SS = Syncopated sequence

Intervals in harmonic sequences

Sequences can be repeated by any interval, up or down, but the most common are:

1. One step lower.

Handel: Gigue from *Xerxes*

2. One step higher.

Kirchhoff: Bourrée

3. A 3rd lower.

Purcell: Minuet from Suite no. 1

4. A 3rd higher.

Mendelssohn: Symphony No. 3 (1st movement)

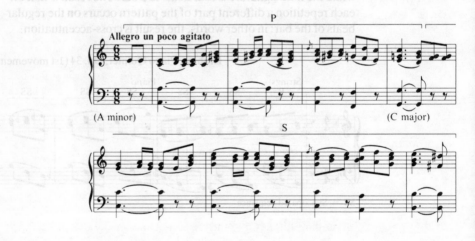

Root movement patterns in sequences

Some of the most common sequence patterns in harmony are:

1. Falling 5ths.

Bach: Minuet from French Suite no. 3

2. Falling 5ths using secondary dominant chords:

Bach: Prelude in F minor from *The Well-tempered Clavier*, Book 2

V^7 of IV   IV^9 V^7 of III   III^9

(A rising 4th is the equivalent of a falling 5th – both go to the same note but at a different octave.)

3. Falling 5ths as far as the roots are concerned, but with one of the chords as a first inversion:

Handel: Fantasia in C

VI II^6 V   I^6 IV VII^6 III VI^6 II V^6

4. Falling 4ths (or rising 5ths):

Chopin: Mazurka in F, Op. 68 no. 3

5. Falling 4ths as far as the roots are concerned, but with one of the chords as a first inversion:

Bach: Gavotte from French Suite no. 5

I   V^6 VI   III^6

WORK ON SEQUENCES IN HARMONY

1. Use the following patterns and add three sequences to each, ending with a cadence.

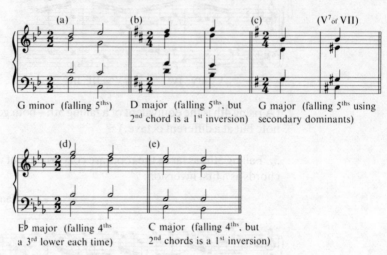

G minor (falling 5^{ths})   D major (falling 5^{ths}, but   G major (falling 5^{ths} using
                                2nd chord is a 1st inversion)   secondary dominants)

E$\flat$ major (falling 4^{ths} C major (falling 4^{ths}, but
a 3rd lower each time)   2nd chords is a 1st inversion)

Play your answers in four different keys

2. Embellish your sequences from exercise **1** in a variety of ways to make more interesting melody and rhythm.

Example:

Decorate each voice in turn, then several voices together. Play the results at the piano.

3. Continue these patterns by adding sequences as indicated.

E major   V$^6_5$ of IV   IV

continue using secondary
dominants as follows:
1st sequence: V$^6_5$ of V - V
2nd sequence: V$^6_5$ of VI - VI

(b) sequences a 3rd lower

F major

(c) sequences a 3rd lower

C major

(d) 2 exact sequences

G major

(e) syncopated sequences one step higher

G major

4. Write a 4-bar pattern followed by two modulating sequences, each of the same length. Start the pattern in A minor, the first sequence in C major and the second sequence in E minor.

5. Write two 8-bar chord progressions (SATB) to illustrate:
a) sequences repeated a tone higher
b) sequences repeated a 3rd higher.

6. Compose a short piece (16–24 bars) for soprano voice with piano accompaniment which makes some use of sequence. You may use these words or make up your own.

I hear thunder.
I hear thunder.
Hark! Don't you?
Hark! Don't you?
Pitter-patter, raindrops,
Pitter-patter, raindrops,
I'm wet through,
So are you.'

(Anon.)

Three-phrase form

A group of three phrases is asymmetrical in design. Each phrase has its own cadence. The first or second phrase may modulate and have a perfect cadence in the new key, but only the third phrase has a full and final perfect cadence in the home (tonic) key. This rounds off the three-phrase form.

The cadences for each phrase of three-phrase form may be arranged in one of these ways.

	Phrase 1	Phrase 2	Phrase 3
Pattern 1	Open (tonic)	Open (tonic)	Perfect (tonic)
Pattern 2	Perfect (new key)	Open	Perfect (tonic)
Pattern 3	Open	Perfect (new key)	Perfect (tonic)

An open cadence is (a) a perfect cadence with the 3rd or 5th of the tonic chord in the top part (this is less final than with the tonic in the top part), or (b) an imperfect cadence, or (c) an interrupted cadence.

The three phrases of this form can also be arranged in three ways.

Type 1	Phrase 1	Phrase 2	Phrase 3
	A1	A2	A3

All three phrases in Type 1 have the same motive(s) as their basis.

American cowboy song: 'Night herding song'

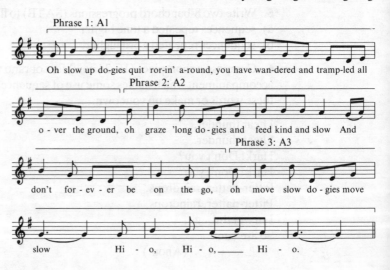

Phrase 1: A1

Oh slow up do-gies quit ror-in' a-round, you have wan-dered and tramp-led all

Phrase 2: A2

o - ver the ground, oh graze 'long do - gies and feed kind and slow And

Phrase 3: A3

don't for - ev - er be on the go, oh move slow do - gies move

slow   Hi - o,   Hi - o,____   Hi - o.

Bach: Cantata no. 208 ('Sheep may safely graze')

Type 2	Phrase 1	Phrase 2	Phrase 3
	A1	A2 (ideas based on A1)	B (new material)
or	A1	B1 (new material)	B2 (ideas based on B1)

Spiritual: 'He never said a mumbalin' word'

Grieg: Norwegian Dance no. 2

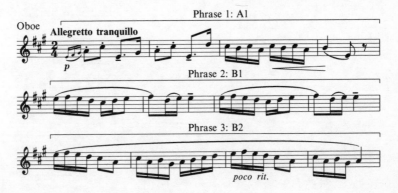

Type 3	Phrase 1	Phrase 2	Phrase 3
	A	B (new material)	C (new material)

This arrangement of three contrasting phrases without repetition allows the composer greater freedom.

Mozart: 'Voi che sapete from *The Marriage of Figaro*

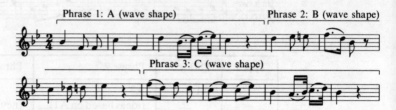

The three contrasting phrases can be held together in a unified way by:

a) A long general melodic curve – arch or bowl shape. (Each phrase in the above example has its own shape, but together these smaller patterns make an overall curve.)

b) A similar accompaniment for all phrases (in the above example, semiquavers).

c) The repeated use of a short rhythmic or intervallic idea.

WORK ON THREE-PHRASE FORM

1. Analyse these three-phrase melodies in the following way:

a) copy out the melody

b) play and sing the melody

c) mark in the phrases

d) state which plan is used (A1,A2,A3; A1,A2,B; A1,B1,B2; or A,B,C)

e) describe the cadences at the end of each phrase as open, perfect in a new key, or perfect in the tonic. The melody notes will help you to decide what the cadences are.

French-Canadian folk song: 'A la claire fontaine'

1.

Spohr: 'Rose, softly blooming'

2.

Somerset folk song: 'O no, John'

3.

Mendelssohn: *Fingal's Cave*

4.

2. Harmonise the melodies from exercise **1** in a suitable style.

3. Compose three-phrase melodies in each of these plans:

(a) A1,A2,A3 (b) A1,A2,B (c) A1,B1,B2 (d) A,B,C (use a broad melodic curve shape to unify the phrases in this plan)

4. Harmonise your melodies from exercise **3** in a suitable style.

CHAPTER NINE

Harmony and modulating melodies

An accidental in a melody can mean one of four things. It could be:

1. A raised or lowered note in a minor key.
2. Part of a secondary dominant chord.
3. A chromatic embellishing note.
4. A sign that the melody modulates.

So how do you know when the accidental points to a change of key – a modulation? It is important to look at:

1. The complete phrase.
2. The melody notes before and those after the accidental.
3. The harmony, if there is any. You have seen how the key or tonality is fixed by root movements and chords.

Play or listen to the start of this piece for piano.

Tchaikovsky: June from *The Seasons*

G minor

The accidentals in the melody of bar 2 are clearly the raised notes of G minor ascending melodic scale.
   Do the accidentals in the next melody suggest a modulation?

Mozart: Piano Sonata in F, K Anhang 135 (1st movement)

F major

The B natural (bar 2) could point to C major but the harmony remains firmly in F major. This note, then, together with the other accidentals in this phrase, is clearly a chromatic embellishing note.
   What of the D sharp accidental (marked with an asterisk) in the next extract?

Schumann: Harvest Song from *Album for the Young*

A major V^7 of V V^7 I

It may at first seem to point to a modulation to the dominant – E major. The chord at the beginning of the next bar, however, cancels out the D sharp, and we find that the chord with the D sharp leads to V^7 of the home key, and is therefore a secondary dominant – V^7 of V.

In the following Air, the accidentals in bars 1 and 2 are raised notes of C melodic minor.

Bach: Air from French Suite no. 2

Eb major   V   I

* = modulating note

It would be easy to think of the B flat and A flat (bar 3) as lowered notes of the home key. But careful study of the harmony shows that the B flat is a modulating note initiating a key change to III (relative major: E flat major).

Similarly, the A natural in the next example could be a chromatic embellishing note, but the harmony at the end of the phrase clearly states a modulation to the dominant. This confirms A natural as a modulating note.

Bach: Gavotte from French Suite no. 4

Eb major   Bb major   V   I

* = modulating note

Implied modulation

Music may sometimes change key even though there are no accidentals in the melody. The melody implies or hints at a modulation. This well-known Christmas song could be harmonised:

1. As a plagal cadence in the tonic key:

Traditional West Country carol: 'A Merry Christmas'

Bb major

IV   I

2. As an imperfect cadence in the tonic key:

IV   V

3. The notes of the melody could hint at a modulation, even without accidentals, to the dominant (F major):

V   I
(F major)

Play and compare the three endings to this phrase. The version which modulates seems to add more interest, colour and contrast to the music.

A key change can take place without using an accidental at all. In the next example the music modulates to B flat major. The bass part clearly outlines a perfect cadence in the new key.

W. F. Bach: Minuet in E flat

Eb major   Bb major V   I

Here are some hints on harmonising melodies which modulate without the use of accidentals.

1. Make a list of the five closely related keys to the tonic.
2. Play or sing through the melody several times.
3. The melody of an implied modulation often moves down to the new tonic note by step.

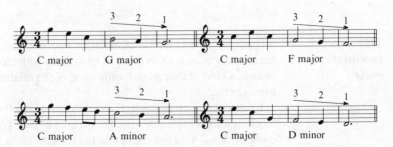

4. Look through the phrase to see if a modulation is suggested by the melody. The new key will be most easily spotted at the cadence point.
5. The last melodic note of the cadence could be 1,3 or 5 of the new tonic chord.
6. Use harmony which will make the new key clear – for example, V—I, V^7–I, I_4^6–V–I.
7. A melody can be harmonised in many different ways. Always look at the final notes of a phrase (especially the second phrase) to see if a modulation to a closely related key is possible.

We can follow these hints through using the first two phrases of this Swiss tune as a model.

Traditional Swiss melody (a) and harmonisation (b)

Phrase 1. There is a clear perfect cadence in the tonic key.
Phrase 2. Suggests a cadence in A major (the dominant) at the end of the phrase because the melody moves down by step to the tonic of the new key (hints 3,4 and 5). Use V–I or V^7–I harmony (hint 6).

It is interesting to note that the modulation is suggested in two further ways:

a) phrase 2 is a sequence of phrase 1 (a 5th higher): the dominant key is a 5th higher than the tonic key
b) the melody in bars 4 and 5 outlines A major – chord I of the new key.

The modulation cycle

So far, you have looked at modulation to one key at a time (except for harmonic sequences). A piece of music may well modulate more than once in a kind of tour round some or all of the related keys from the tonic centre.

Composers such as Bach, Handel, Mozart, Beethoven, and some modern song writers often use the cycle of keys to good effect in their compositions. You will recall that the tonic key is at the centre of its related keys. The dominant and its relative major or relative minor key are on the bright, sharp side of the tonic. The subdominant and its relative major or relative minor key are nicely balanced on the darker, flat side of the tonic.

Music which moves through more than one key usually follows these stages:

Stage 1. Establish the tonic key.
Stage 2. Modulate to and establish with a cadence the second key. The second key is often V if the tonic is major, or III if the tonic is minor. This is the most important modulation.
Stage 3. Move through other related keys. These modulations are usually quicker and on the flat, darker side of the tonic. Sequences can be very useful in this stage.
Stage 4. Return to the tonic key and end with a perfect cadence. Follow these stages through in this Bourrée.

Handel: Bourrée from *Water Music*

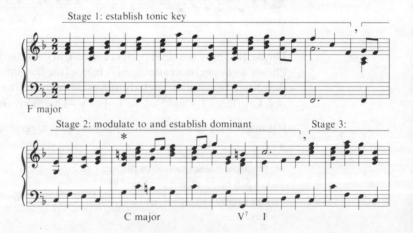

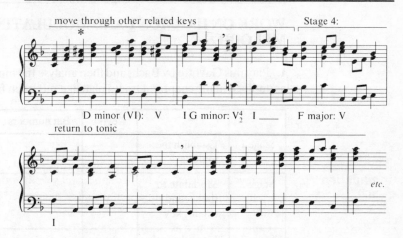

* = modulating note

As you will see in future chapters, the modulation cycle is used in many pieces in two- and three-part forms.

WORK ON HARMONY AND MODULATING MELODIES

1. Play this Gavotte by Bach, and then analyse the modulation cycle as outlined in the chapter. Draw a plan like this, then fill in the details

		Key(s)	Bar numbers	Cadence
Stage 1	Establish the tonic key			
Stage 2	Modulate to the second (main) key			
Stage 3	Move through other related keys			
Stage 4	Return to the tonic			

Bach: Gavotte from English Suite no. 3

2. Play these melodies, then harmonise each in the style of the opening. Look for implied modulations in the melody. There are some ideas to help you in the chapter.

18th-century melody: *Adeste fideles*

Loeillet: Minuet from Suite in G minor

Bach: chorale *Ach wie flüchtig, ach wie nichtig*

(two modulations)

3. Compose five melodies of between 8 and 12 bars long. Include implied modulations (without using accidentals) to the following keys. Return to the tonic key at the end.

Melody 1: D major to A major (dominant) and back.

Melody 2: E flat major to C minor (relative minor) and back.

Melody 3: F major to G minor (II, relative minor of the subdominant) and back.

Melody 4: G major to C major (subdominant) and back.

Melody 5: F sharp minor to D major (VI, relative major of the subdominant) and back.

4. Harmonise two melodies from exercise 3.

5. Compose a short piece for piano (16–24 bars) which modulates to at least three closely related keys. Use the four-stage plan suggested in the chapter. Your analysis from exercise 1 may also help in this task.

Four-phrase plans

In music of four or more phrases, some sort of plan or form is needed to keep a sense of unity in the music.

The four phrases can be arranged in one of these ways.

Plan 1	Phrase 1	Phrase 2	Phrase 3	Phrase 4
	A1	A2	A3	A4

All phrases are developed from one motive and this provides unity.

No two cadences are exactly the same. Only the final phrase has a full and final perfect cadence (tonic note in the melody).

Traditional Scottish melody: 'Scots, wha' hae'

Plan 2	Group 1		Group 2	
	Phrase 1	Phrase 2	Phrase 3	Phrase 4
	A1	A2	A1	A3
Cadences	often V—1 (3rd or 5th at top)	imperfect	often V–I (3rd or 5th at top)	final V–I (tonic at top)

This plan has two parallel groups, each of two balanced and symmetrical phrases. Both groups start in the same way. Phrases 2 and 4 may be similar to, or contrast with, phrases 1 and 3.

Chopin: Mazurka in G minor, Op. 24 no. 1

Plan 3	Group 1		Group 2	
	Phrase 1	Phrase 2	Phrase 3	Phrase 4
	A1	B1	A2	B2
Cadences	often V—1 (3rd or 5th at top)	imperfect	often V–I (3rd or 5th at top)	final V–I (tonic at top)
		contrasts with A1		contrasts with A2

This plan has two parallel groups, each comprising two balanced, symmetrical, but contrasting phrases.

American ballad: 'The streets of Laredo'

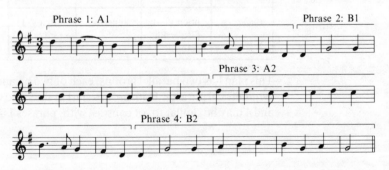

Plan 4	Group 1		Group 2	
	Phrase 1	Phrase 2	Phrase 3	Phrase 4
	A1	A2	B	C
Cadences	often V—1 (3rd or 5th at top)	imperfect	often V–I (3rd or 5th at top)	final V–I (tonic at top)

The two groups start in a different way.

Traditional English melody: 'The meeting of the waters'

Other plans   1. Four contrasting phrases – A, B, C, D.

16th-century English melody: 'Callino castureme'

2. Five-phrase melody – A1, B1, B2, A2, A3.

Traditional English melody: 'The meeting of the waters'

WORK ON FOUR-PHRASE PLANS

1. Analyse the following four-phrase melodies in this way:

a) copy out the melody

b) play and sing the melody several times

c) mark in the phrases

d) state which plan is used (refer back to the chapter if you need to)

e) describe the cadences at the end of each phrase. The melody notes will help you to decide what the cadences are.

Prokofiev: *Cortège de sauterelles* ('The grasshoppers' procession')

Camidge: Piano Sonata no. 1 in G (2nd movement)

Traditional Scottish melody: 'Annie Laurie'

2. Harmonise the melodies from exercise **1** in a suitable style.

3. Compose a four-phrase melody according to each of these plans:
(a) A1, A2, A3, A4   (d) A1, A2, B, C
(b) A1, A2, A1, A3   (e) A, B, C, D
(c) A1, B1, A2, B2

Use a broad curve shape, similar rhythm or similar intervals to help unify plan (e).

4. Compose a five-phrase melody in the plan: A1, B1, B2, A2, A3.

5. Harmonise three melodies from exercises **3** and **4**.

CHAPTER TEN

The diminished seventh chord

The diminished 7th chord is made up of three minor 3rds. It appears as a diatonic chord (VII^{d7}) in the harmonic minor scale.

C minor: VII^{d7}

Diminished 7ths are very active and restless chords because they have:

1. Three active notes – the root, 3rd and 7th:

2. Two diminished intervals:

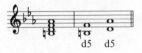

Three inversions are possible:

Inversions of diminished 7th chords

Play the inversions and you will notice that they all sound the same as harmony. This is because all intervals are always the same size – three semitones each apart. Their effect in music can be different, however. For example, a root position moves more strongly to the next chord than does a second inversion.

Approach and resolution

Approach and resolve the diminished 7th chord as you would other 7th chords. The most usual approach is by step or stop. The most usual resolution of the active intervals (d5 and d7) is by step to notes of the tonic triad. Play and study these examples in C minor.

VII^{d7}   VII^{d7}   VII₅⁶

VII₃⁴   VII₂⁴

↗ ↘ = by step
---- = by stop

For a less smooth effect, approach the diminished 7th by a leap.

VII^{d7}

Note:
In four-part writing all notes of the chord are generally used.

**Uses of
Diminished
7th chords**

Composers began regularly to use this colourful chord for dramatic effects in the 18th century. It became very popular in the late 19th century with composers such as Wagner, Liszt and Tchaikovsky. At times the chord has been used rather too much and its effect has correspondingly lessened. The diminished 7th is, however, a useful chord which can be used to good effect in a number of ways. Here are some examples:

1. VII^{d7} as a dark, dominant-type chord moving to I or V:

Bach: aria 'Have mercy, Lord' from *St Matthew Passion*

B minor   VII₅⁶   VII^{d7}   I

VII^{d7} is heard here first as an inversion, then in root position moving to I. It illustrates the word 'trouble' with a dark quality.

2. VII^{d7} as a secondary dominant chord moving strongly to V (or I$^6_4$–V):

Schumann: *Die beiden Grenadiere*, Op. 49

Set   free   from their dark   Rus - sian   pri - son;

G minor   VII$^4_3$ V^6

VII^{d7} can also act as a secondary dominant of II, III, IV and VI. Here are just two examples:

Verdi: Miserere from *Il trovatore*

(a)

D minor

VII^{d7}of IV   IV

Verdi: 'Il balen del suo sorriso' from *Il trovatore*

(b)   *

B♭ major

∗ = VII^{d7}of II

3. VII^{d7} as a chromatic passing chord.

a) VII^{d7} of V between IV and V:

Bach: chorale *Herzliebster Jesu*

B minor

* = VII^{d7}of V

b) VII^{d7} of II between I and II:

Reger: *Fast zu Keck*, Op. 17 no. 12

C major

* = VII^{d7}of II

c) VII^{d7} of VI between V and VI:

Beethoven: Piano Sonata in A, Op. 101 (1st movement)

A major

* = VII^{d7}of VI

4. VII^{d7} as a forceful, sudden surprise or climax:

Bach: Prelude in B flat minor from *The Well-tempered Clavier*, Book 1

5. VII^{d7} with decorated appoggiaturas (especially in arpeggio writing for the keyboard):

Bach: Chromatic Fantasy

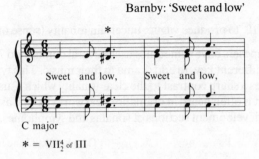

D minor   VII$\frac{4}{3}$ of V   VII$\frac{4}{3}$ of IV   VII$\frac{4}{3}$ of V

* = appoggiatura

6. VII^{d7} as a rich and distinctive chord in close harmony:

Barnby: 'Sweet and low'

Sweet and low,   Sweet and low,

C major

* = VII$\frac{4}{2}$ of III

7. VII^{d7} (like V or V⁷) as a chord which modulates.
a) by moving straight into the new key:

Brahms: Waltz in D minor, Op. 39 no. 9

Andante espressivo

p

VII^{d7}

D minor: VII^{d7} of IV
G minor: VII^{d7}   I

b) by moving to V then I of the new key:

Brahms: Waltz in D minor, Op. 39 no. 9

(F major)   D minor: VII$_5^6$ of V

(D minor) V$_5^6$ I   II$_5^6$ V

8. VII^{d7} to produce vague, uncertain tonality (sense of key).

Composers have sometimes used several diminished 7th chords, each in a different key, to add drama to their music. This type of writing makes a sharp contrast to the clear tonality which usually follows. The effect is often heard in dramatic vocal works as well as introductions and development sections of sonatas and symphonies.

Tchaikovsky: June from *The Seasons*

G major   VII$_5^6$ VII$_2^4$ VII^{d7} VII$_3^4$ VII$_3^4$ VII$_5^6$ VII$_3^4$
                      of III of VI   of VI   of II of IV of V   of V

WORK ON THE DIMINISHED 7th CHORD

1. Write diminished 7th chords (root position, 1st, 2nd and 3rd inversions) in these keys:
(a) A minor
(b) D minor
(c) F sharp minor
(d) F minor

2. Add approach and resolution chords to each of the diminished 7ths you have written in exercise **1.** Move mainly by step or stop and write for SATB.

3. The following extracts illustrate one or more of the musical uses of diminished 7th chords. Copy out and play each example; then:
a) describe the function of the chord
b) write symbols underneath the stave to analyse the chords.

Mozart: Piano Sonata in C minor, K 457 (1st movement)

Mozart: An die Einsamkeit

Schubert: Piano Sonata in A, D 664 (1st movement)

Mozart: Piano Sonata in C minor, K 457 (3rd movement)

4. Write a progression of chords for SATB (decorated where necessary) to illustrate:

a) VII^{d7} as a secondary dominant moving to I$^6_4$ then V in G minor

b) VII^{d7} of II as a chromatic passing chord between I and II in B minor

c) VII^{d7} in a forceful climax (C minor)

d) VII^{d7} decorated with appoggiaturas and arpeggios (C sharp minor)

e) VII^{d7} as a modulating chord

f) VII^{d7} as a dominant-type chord

5. Compose a song of 24 bars in *close* harmony for a 'barber shop' quartet of male voices. Use three different diminished 7th chords in a variety of inversions.

6. Compose a ländler of 16 bars for piano. Include diminished 7th chords in a variety of roles (for example, decorated and as chromatic passing chords, secondary dominants, climax chords). (A ländler is an Austrian dance rather like a slow waltz.)

Two-part form

So far you have looked at different phrase plans with a full, complete perfect cadence only at the end of the last phrase. (A full perfect cadence is where the soprano or top line comes to rest on the tonic note.) Plans using the full perfect cadence only once are called one-part forms. Two-part form (sometimes called 'binary' form) was popular in early dance music. The two sections allow the music more space to develop. Although the second section often uses ideas from the first, the two are never exactly the same. Each section ends with a perfect cadence. In simple two-part form both cadences are often in the tonic key. In more extended two-part form, section one may end with a perfect cadence in the dominant or relative major key.

Types of two-part form

1. Short two-part form.

Part 1	Part 2 [sometimes longer]
Phrase 1 .... perfect cadence	Phrase 2 .... perfect cadence

English folk song: 'Mister Frog's wedding'

Sometimes one part or phrase is repeated:

Traditional: *The Boar's Head Carol*

The most common arrangement repeats both parts:

Traditional: 'Let Erin remember'

2. Parallel two-part form.

Part 1	Part 2 [uses the same motive as 1 but in a varied way and/ or different key]
Section A1 .... perfect cadence	Section A2 .... perfect cadence

Traditional Scottish melody: *Auld Lang Syne*

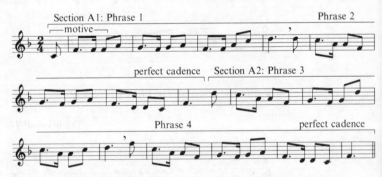

3. Contrasted two-part form.

Part 1	Part 2 [Starts with a different tune, but often ends in the same way as A1. This helps to unify the music.]
Section A1 .... perfect cadence	Section B1 .... perfect cadence

Spiritual: 'Liza Jane'

4. Extended two-part form.

Part 1	Part 2
Section 1:	Section 2:
Phrase A – tonic key	Phrase C – tonic key
Phrase B – modulates to V in major; III in minor	(or passes through tonic and other related keys)
	Phrase D – tonic (sometimes to related key(s))
perfect cadence	perfect cadence in tonic

Mozart: Minuet composed at five years of age

Note these points about extended two-part form:

a) The same motive is often used throughout (perhaps in different ways and different keys).

b) Part 2 is often longer than Part 1.
c) The music passes through several of the closely related keys. There is no set plan for this, but modulation is often first to a brighter key (V from a major key, V or III from a minor key). The darker keys (IV or II from a major key, IV or VI from a minor key) usually appear in Part 2.
d) Extended two-part form makes it possible to treat a motive in a tight, organized and interesting way.

WORK ON TWO-PART FORM

1. Write out and play through these examples of two-part form.
Mark on your copy of these examples:
a) details of the two parts (including smaller phrases)
b) where the cadences occur
c) the type of two-part form used (for example, simple or contrasted)

Medieval students' song: *Gaudeamus igitur*

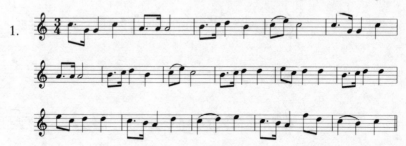

Traditional American song: 'Yankee Doodle'

Hook: Minuet from *Guida di musica*, Op. 37

2. Analyse this example of extended two-part form by marking on your copy details of:

a) the two parts (including the number of phrases)
b) motive(s)
c) the modulation scheme
d) cadences
e) melodic shape

Bach: Gavotte from Orchestral Suite no. 3

3. Develop these melodic motives into two-part form as indicated.

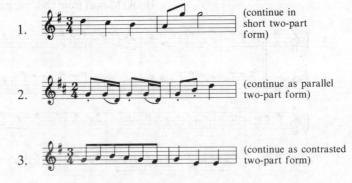

1. (continue in short two-part form)

2. (continue as parallel two-part form)

3. (continue as contrasted two-part form)

4. (continue as short two-part form, both phrases repeated)

5.  (extended two-part form, passing through D minor and F major in Part 2; end Part 1 with a perfect cadence in C major)

4. Compose a piece of 20 bars for harpsichord in extended two-part form. Part 1 should be 8 bars and Part 2, 12 bars long. Pass through several related keys. Develop your motive(s)/ideas in a variety of ways.

CHAPTER ELEVEN

Harmony and the chorale

A chorale is a hymn tune of the Lutheran Church. These German melodies were harmonised by many composers during the 16th, 17th and 18th centuries. At first, chorales were quite free in rhythm.

Hassler: 'Herzlich tut mich verlangen' from *Lustgarten neuer Teutscher Gesäng*

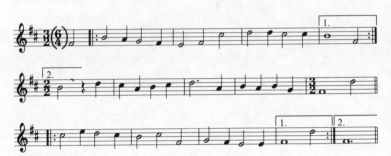

By the 18th century the chorale had become more symmetrical in shape.

Bach sometimes harmonised the same chorale in several different ways. Here is just one of his nine settings of this well-known melody, sometimes called the Passion Chorale.

Bach: Passion Chorale from *St Matthew Passion*

Features of the chorale

1. Chorale melody is simple, slow and dignified – about $\quarternote = 60$.
2. Chorales start and end in the same key.
3. Each phrase ends in a cadence.
4. Chorales are for voices – music to be sung – so should be written within the range for each voice.
5. Every word is sung by each voice (SATB), though not always at the same time, since one part may sing a word or syllable in advance of or following the other parts.
6. You may, by using embellishing notes, have more than one note to a word or syllable.

Bach's chorale harmonisations

Bach was a master of chorale harmonisation. It is almost impossible to match his mastery of chorale setting, and this is not the purpose of your task. By careful study of Bach's examples you will gain an insight into his great imagination and wealth of ideas.

There are several published collections of Bach chorale harmonisations. Some chorales appear in hymn books and also in the great choral works such as the *St Matthew Passion*. It is important that you play, sing and study as many examples as possible. Here are just a few of Bach's 'thumbprints' to help you on your way.

1. Bach's harmony ranges from gentle, simple, diatonic chords to more active, chromatic and dissonant sounds (diminished 7ths, secondary dominants, etc.). The style he uses is often suggested by the meaning of the words. Here are two short examples:

Bach: harmonisations of the Passion Chorale melody

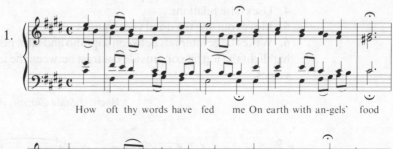

How oft thy words have fed me On earth with an-gels' food

And when my heart must lan - guish In

death's last aw - ful throe.

The words of the first example describe a simple respect for God, and the harmony uses simple diatonic chords. Compare this with the harmony of the second example, using the same melody but with different words and mood. Rich chromatic and dissonant chords are used to illustrate the sadness of the words.

2. Bach's part-writing is often more active than the melody, freely using embellishing notes and suspensions.

3. When one or two parts are active the other parts move more simply.

4. Soprano and bass parts generally have the most interesting melodic shape; alto and tenor are usually smooth and flowing.

5. Cadences are striking, clearly marked, varied and in different keys.

6. Root movements are mainly strong, especially towards cadences.

7. Chorales have at least one modulation; some have several.

Bach was always concerned with the melodic and rhythmic interest of each vocal line. This, together with his interest in rich harmony and word-painting, led him to change some of the more traditional methods of part-writing. For example, he sometimes:

1. Doubles the 3rd of a chord (even the leading note) for a richer sound.

2. Moves the leading note down a 3rd in a perfect cadence to the 5th of the tonic chord. Sometimes the leading note moves up a 4th to the 3rd of the tonic chord.

3. Crosses and/or overlaps parts.

4. Uses false relations.

5. Moves outside the usual vocal ranges.

6. Writes large intervals between soprano and alto, perhaps to highlight the top line or provide contrast between the upper and lower voices.

Bach: chorale *Christie, du Lamm Gottes*

Lamb of God, our Sa - viour

Who our sins dost take a - way,   Have mer - cy

Bach: chorale *Valet will ich dir geben*

When playing and singing the chorales, notice also the way Bach:

7. Harmonises repeated notes with turning patterns and falling or rising bass lines.

8. Uses the same chord across the bar line, sometimes with the bass leaping an octave.

9. Introduces the subdominant key (by lowering the leading note of the home key) towards the end of the chorale.

10. Prefers II⁶₅ to IV at cadence points.

A method for harmonising chorales

1. Play and sing (with the words) the melody. What sort of mood do the words suggest?

Bach: chorale Nun danket alle Gott

Now thank we all our God, with heart and hands and
Who wond-rous things hath done, In whom His world re-

voi - ces, Who from our moth-er's arms Hath bless'd us on our
joi - ces:

way With count-less gifts of love, And still is ours to-day.

2. Try to match the style of your part-writing and harmony with the feeling or mood of the text. Words like 'dark', 'death', 'sorrow' and 'bitter' may suggest active and dissonant harmony or dark keys. 'Joy', 'strong', 'risen' and 'praise' may suggest strong, simple and bright chords and keys. Think also of the general mood suggested by the text. This chorale is obviously joyful and bright.

3. Pay careful attention to cadences. Look for examples of two-part form or phrase-group patterns. In chorales, Part 1 often ends with a perfect cadence (tonic key). Part 2 can have several varied cadences. Try to use a full perfect cadence (tonic in the soprano) only at the end of the final phrase.

4. Rough in the outline of the cadences – these are strong and basic.

5. Complete the bass part.

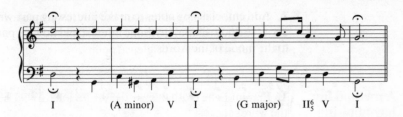

I   (A minor) V   I   (G major) II$_5^6$ V   I

6. Add the remaining harmony in block chords.

(G major) I   I   I^6 IV   IV   I   VI^6 V$_5^6$ I   V   I

(G major) V   I   V   V   V   I   I   V   V
           (D major) I   IV   VI   II^7 V

(D major) I   IV   (G major) I^6 V   I IV^6 II$_5^6$ V   I
 (G major) I   IV   II
  (A minor) I III VII I   V   I

7. Add embellishing notes to make interesting part-writing. Think about melodic shape, rhythmic interest and flowing parts in relation to the mood of the words.

Now thank we all our God, With heart and hands and
Who wond-rous things hath done, In whom His world re-

voi - ces, Who from our moth-er's arms Hath bless'd us on our
joi - ces:

way With countless gifts of love, And still is ours to - day.

8. Always be prepared to change your ideas as you tackle each of the above stages. Re-write where necessary to improve shape and part-writing.

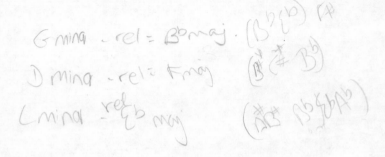

WORK ON HARMONY AND THE CHORALE

1. Play through the different stages of chorale harmonisation in the chapter. Write a bar-by-bar analysis of any embellishments added to the final version. Lay out your answer like this:

Bar	Beat	Voice	Embellishment
1	1	Bass	Unaccented passing note

2. Play and sing these two harmonisations of the same chorale tune by Bach. Then:
a) analyse the harmonies
b) list the embellishments used
c) compare the words of each setting. Say how you think the words have influenced the style of harmony Bach has written.

Bach: chorale *Herzliebster Jesu*

Bach: chorale *Herzliebster Jesu* as it appears in the *St Matthew Passion*

3. Harmonise (for SATB) each of these phrases in two different ways. Think about the words and how these might suggest a particular style or styles for your harmony.

Bach: chorale *Allein Gott in der Höh' sei Ehr'*

Bach: chorale *Aus tiefer Not screi ich zu dir*

Bach: chorale *Der Tag, der ist so freudenreich*

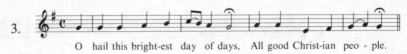

3.

O hail this bright-est day of days, All good Christ-ian peo - ple.

Bach: chorale *O Lamm Gottes, unschuldig*

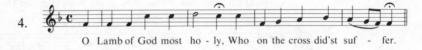

4.

O Lamb of God most ho - ly, Who on the cross did'st suf - fer.

4. Add parts for alto and tenor to complete the harmony for these chorales.

Bach: chorale *Wie schön leuchtet der Morgenstern*

1.

O Morn - ing Star! how fair and bright Thou
Thou Root of Jes - se, Da - vid's son, My

beam-est forth in truth and light! O Sov-reign meek and
Lord and Bride-groom, Thou hast won My heart to serve Thee

low - ly Ho - ly art Thou, Fair and Glor-ious All vic - tor-ious
sole - ly!

Rich in bles - sing, Rule and might o'er all pos - ses - sing.

Bach: chorale *Komm, Gott Schöpfer, heiliger Geist*

2.

Come, O Cre-a-tor Spi-rit blest! And in our Souls take up Thy rest; Come

with Thy grace and heav'n-ly aid, To fill the hearts which Thou hast made

5. Harmonise these chorale tunes for SATB in the style of Bach.

Bach: chorale *Liebster Jesu, wir sind hier*

1.

Blessed Jesu, at Thy word
We are gathered all to hear thee;
Let our hearts and souls be raised
Now to seek and love and fear thee;
By thy teaching sweet and holy
Drawn from earth to love thee solely.

Bach: chorale *Vater unser im Himmelreich*

2.

Our Father, Thou in heaven above,
Who biddest us to dwell in love,
As brethren of one family,
And cry for all we need to Thee,
Teach us to mean the words we say,
And from the inmost heart to pray.

6. Compare your workings from exercises **4** and **5** with Bach's originals.

Three-part form

Three-part form, or ternary form as it is sometimes called, appears in many short pieces – songs, Romantic piano pieces (for example, nocturnes, rhapsodies, intermezzos). It is also used in longer movements for orchestra.

Each of the three sections is about the same length. Parts 1 and 3 are the same or similar, but Part 2 provides a contrast.

Part 1	Part 2	Part 3
Statement	Contrast	Restatement or return of Part 1

The cadences for each part are arranged like this:

Part 1	Part 2	Part 3
Perfect cadence in tonic or related key	Imperfect cadence in tonic or perfect cadence in a related key	Perfect cadence in tonic key

Types of three-part form

1. Simple: one phrase or group of phrases, in each part.

Phrase 1	Phrase 2	Phrase 3
A1	B	A2

Spiritual: 'Deep river'

2. First part repeated.

Part 1	Part 2	Part 3
‖: A1 :‖	B	A2

Traditional Welsh melody: 'All through the night'

3. Small three-part form: the most common plan. Part 1 is repeated, and parts 2 and 3 are repeated together.

Part 1	Part 2	Part 3
‖: A1 :‖	‖: B	A2 :‖

Hook: Minuet from *Guida di musica*, Op. 37

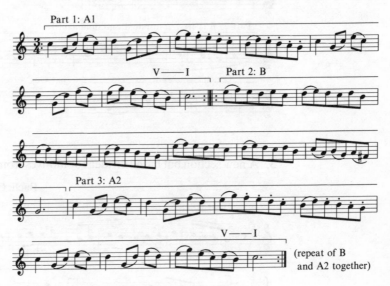

Part 1: A1

V——I   Part 2: B

Part 3: A2

V——I

(repeat of B and A2 together)

Part 2 (B) of three-part form can be:

1. A new melody:

Tchaikovsky: *Old French Song*, Op. 39 no. 16

Part 1: A1

Part 2: B (new melody)

[Part 3: A2 (= repeated A1)]

2. Part 1 (A) transposed into a different key for contrast:

Schumann: *Humming Song*, Op. 68 no. 3

3. A new section but based on ideas or motives from Part 1 (A):

Bach: Gavotte in G minor

4. A short development section which may use motives or rhythmic, melodic or harmonic ideas from Part 1 (A). The music may pass through several keys, use faster harmonic rhythm, sequence, inversion, augmentation, diminution, and so on.

Mozart: Piano Sonata in B flat (Minuet)

Part I: A1

Part 2: B

Part 3: A2

Part 3 (A2) is often an exact repetition of Part 1 (A1). You may even see 'da capo' at the end of Part 2 (B). This means simply repeat Part 1 from the beginning. Part 3 may also be a varied version of Part 1, but still easily identified as Part 1.

Schumann: *Little Folk Song*, Op. 68 no. 9

WORK ON THREE-PART FORM

1. Write out and play through these examples of three-part form:
Mark on your copy:

a) details of the three parts (including smaller phrases)

b) the cadences

c) the type of three-part form used – Model 1: simple; Model 2: Part 1
   repeated; or Model 3: Parts 2 and 3 repeated together.

Spiritual: 'Roll, Jordan, roll'

Traditional Welsh melody: *The Ash Grove*

Haydn: Piano Sonata in D, Hob. XVI: 14 (Minuet)

3.

2. Analyse this example of small three-part form by marking on your copy details of:

a) the three parts
b) motives
c) the modulation scheme
d) cadences
e) melodic shape

Blow: English Air

3. Develop these melodic motives into three-part form as indicated

Mozart: Piano Sonata in E flat, K 282 (Minuet)

1.  Model 1 - use a
new melody for B

Bruckner: Symphony No. 4 (2nd movement)

Andante

2.  Model 2 - transpose
A1 into a new key for B

Scarlatti: Sonata in D minor, no. 413

3.

Model 3 - B should be a short
development section moving through
3 different, related, keys
and developing ideas from A1

4. Compose a song (with piano accompaniment) of 24 bars in small three-part form. Pass through a number of keys and develop your original motive(s).

You may use these words or make up some of your own.

How sweet this morning air in Spring,
When tender is the grass, and wet!
I see some little leaves have not
Outgrown their early childhood yet;
And cows no longer hurry home,
However sweet a voice cries 'Come'!
(*Early Spring* by W.H. Davies)

CHAPTER TWELVE

Lake (19th →

Ninth chords — colourful

Add a 3rd to a 7th chord and you will have a chord of five notes – a 9th chord. The most common 9th chord is the dominant 9th. The 9th may be major or minor.

(It is interesting to note that 9th chords, like 7th chords, are a natural grouping of overtones in the harmonic series. The above chord has the overtones 4,5,6,7 and 9 of G.)

9th chords were especially popular in 19th-century Romantic music and 20th-century Impessionism; they also occur frequently in the popular song-writing of today.

Uses of the dominant 9th

The 9th may be used melodically or harmonically.

1. As an embellishment (often an appoggiatura or auxiliary note). The 9th moves down by step (to the dominant) before the chord itself resolves.

Spiritual: 'Were you there?'

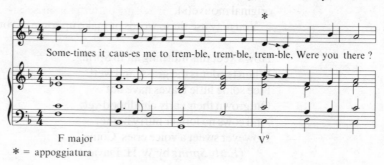

Some-times it caus-es me to trem-ble, trem-ble, trem-ble, Were you there ?

F major   V⁹

* = appoggiatura

2. As a rich chord, and one more colourful than V or V⁷.

Beethoven: Piano Concerto No. 3 (1st movement)

C minor: V   V⁷   V⁹

3. By the same token, as a more tense, expressive and dissonant dominant chord.

Schubert: Symphony No. 9 (1st movement)

4. Melodically, as a broken chord for special, dramatic effects. It is used here as a falling pattern to highlight the word 'grief':

Bach: Chorus no. 78 from *St Matthew Passion*

and in this example in a rising pattern for 'arise':

Mendelssohn: *Elijah*

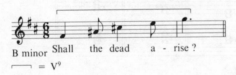

Notice in the above examples that the minor 9th is more dissonant than the major 9th. Both are discordant, but the major 9th has a brighter sound, the minor 9th is darker and more gloomy.

Part-writing hints

1. Since the dominant 9th has five notes, at least one note must be left out in four-part writing. The 5th is usually omitted as this is the least important of all the notes.

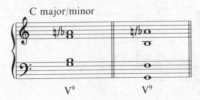

Play these chords and you will hear that the sound is rather thin when the 3rd or the 7th is left out.

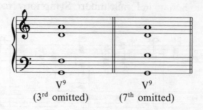

V^9 V^9
(3rd omitted)   (7th omitted)

2. The 9th is often in the top part. When it appears in an inside part it is usually a 9th or more from the root.

Wagner: *Götterdämmerung*

F major
* = major 9th

Some 20th-century composers write all the notes of 9th chords close together. This is called a chord cluster. Play these arrangements of a 9th chord and notice how the quality of the chord changes when spaced differently.

C major

Chord cluster

3. The 9th of V^9 chords can be prepared in the previous chord or need not be prepared at all.

4. The 9th usually moves:
a) down by step

Beethoven: Piano Sonata in E minor, Op. 90 (1st movement)

E minor
V^9

b) by a step or leap to another note of the chord.

Beethoven: Piano Sonata in E minor, Op. 90 (1st movement)

E minor

V^9

Inversion of 9th chords

9th chords have four inversions:

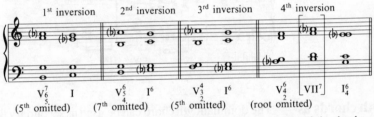

1st inversion	2nd inversion	3rd inversion	4th inversion
V^7_6 ⁵ I	V^6_5 ⁴ I^6	V^4_3 ₂ I^6	V^6_4 ₂ VII⁷ I^6_4
(5th omitted)	(7th omitted)	(5th omitted)	(root omitted)

Flats have been added in parentheses to show the minor versions of the chords.

The 4th inversion is not often used in traditional music as the 9th would have to be below the root. It is sometimes heard in 20th-century music. If the root is left out the chord is the same as VII⁷ and its inversions. Used without its root, the 4th inversion of V⁹ does, however, give a strong feel of V–I harmony.

Use of 9th chord inversions

1. As a first inversion:

Lalo: *Symphonie espagnole*, Op. 21 (4th movement)

Andante

ppp

D minor: I   ³ V^7_6 ⁵   I   ³

2. As a second inversion:

Schubert: Waltz in D, Op. 33 no. 2

D major: V$^6_{4/3}$ V^9 I

3. As a third inversion:

Schumann: A Curious Story from *Scenes of Childhood*, Op. 15 no. 2

D major: V$^4_{3/2}$ I^6

9th chords as secondary dominants

The dominant 9th chord can be used as secondary dominant. For example:

1. V^9 of V:

Franck: Symphony in D minor (3rd movement)

D major V^9 of V   V^9 V^9 of V   V^9

2. V^9 of IV:

Bach: Prelude in F minor from *The Well-tempered Clavier*, Book 1

F minor V^9 of IV _____ IV   V   IV^6 V I   V

9th chords on other degrees of the scale

Like secondary 7ths, 9th chords can be used on other degrees of the scale. II⁹ and IV⁹ are the most common.

Debussy: 'La fille aux cheveux de lin' from *Préludes*, Book 1

Gb major   II⁹   V⁹   II⁹

Puccini: *La Bohème*

F minor   I   IV⁹

9th chord patterns

Here is a pattern of 9th chords moving to common chords:

C major   V⁹ I IV⁹ VII III⁹ VI II⁹ V I⁹ IV VII⁹ III VI⁹ II V⁹ I

9th chords may move to other 9th chords:

C major   II⁹   V⁹   I⁹   IV⁹   VII⁹   III⁹   VI⁹   II⁹   V⁹   I

9th chords may move in parallel:

Debussy: *Pelléas et Mélisande*

WORK ON 9th CHORDS

1. Write, play and sing dominant 9th chords in root, 1st, 2nd, 3rd and 4th inversions, in these keys:

Major keys: G, A, F, B flat, A flat

Minor keys: E, F sharp, D, B, G

2. Re-write the chords from exercise **1** for SATB. (You will need to omit one of the chord notes, usually the 5th.)

Prepare and resolve each of the above chords. The 9th may move down by step or to another note of the same chord.

3. Copy, play and analyse the 9th chords in these extracts (which may be dominant or secondary 9ths).

a) write chord symbols under the stave for all chords

b) state whether the 9th is used melodically or harmonically (for example, as an embellishment, rich chord, broken chord)

c) say how the 9th is prepared and resolved

d) say which note(s) of the chord is omitted, if any.

Haydn: Quartet in G, Op. 76 (1st movement)

1.

G major

Haydn: Quartet in F minor, *Trautwein* no. 3 (4th movement), Op. 25 no. 5

2.

F minor

Tchaikovsky: June from *The Seasons*

3.

Andante cantabile

G minor

Chopin: Nocturne in G minor, Op. 15 no. 3

F♯ major

4. Write 8 bars for SATB in B minor. Include examples of (a) a dominant 9th in root position, (b) V^9 as a secondary dominant (either V^9 of V, or V^9 of IV) and (c) II^9.

5. Write a sequence pattern of 9th chords moving to common chords in G major and $\frac{6}{8}$ time (see chapter). Decorate your answer with embellishments (in the soprano, alto or tenor part) to make the pattern melodically and rhythmically interesting.

6. Compose a piece of 16 bars for piano in common time ($\frac{4}{4}$) in B flat major. Include part or all of the sequence pattern of 9th chords moving to other 9th chords (see chapter).

7. Harmonise these melodies using the occasional 9th chord where appropriate.

Spiritual: 'I got a robe'

I got a robe, You got a robe, All God's chil-lun got a robe   When I get to Hea-b'n goin-a put on my robe, goin-a shout all o-ber God's Hea-b'n, ___ Hea-b'n, ___ Hea-b'n, ___ Ev-'ry-bo-dy talk-in' 'bout Hea-b'n ain't go-in' there Hea-b'n, ___ Hea-b'n, ___ goin-a shout all o-ber God's Hea-b'n. ___

Gurlitt: Serenade, Op. 172 no. 5

* = chromatic notes

8. Compose a piece for piano which makes some use of 9th chords in both melody and harmony. Use some of the following types of 9th chord: root position and inversion chords, chord clusters, V^9 as a secondary dominant or parallel 9ths.

Melody from harmony

In some compositions, melody is designed around an existing bass line or set pattern of chords. In other words, the harmony was composed before the melody.

Well-known basses

One dance of the 16th and 17th centuries, called the passamezzo, used a set chord pattern as a basis for its composition. The following well-known tune was composed to the passamezzo chord sequence.

Traditional melody: *Greensleeves*
Passamezzo chord pattern

More recently, the 12-bar blues follows a very similar pattern of chords, although jazz chords often have 7ths and other notes added for a richer texture. Jazz performers use the 12-bar sequence as a framework for improvising blues melody. 'Blue' notes are chromatic (outside the key) – the 3rd and 7th are often flattened in a descending scale pattern.

12-bar blues pattern

Simple 12-bar blues

A bass line which is repeated throughout a composition is called a ground bass. Other variations on a bass line include the passacaglia and chaconne. The chaconne has a fixed chord pattern with its own rhythm which is repeated for each variation.

Variations

Johann Pachelbel (1653–1706), a German composer, composed thirteen variations based on the repeated chord pattern of this chaconne – a short, slow dance in triple time.

Pachelbel: *Ciaconna* with 13 variations

Let us look at a few of the variations to see how Pachelbel has used these simple chords as a basis for different ideas.

Variation 1: simple decoration (using auxiliary and passing notes, etc.) – bars 1–4 in the right hand, bars 5–8 in the left hand.

Variation 2: broken chord patterns in quavers in the right hand.

Variation 6: dotted note patterns (right hand). The left hand links chord roots together with passing notes.

Variation 7: right hand in parallel 6ths and 3rds. Left hand has chord roots.

Variation 8: broken chord patterns between both hands. The chord is sounded on the third beat of each bar.

Variation 11: Descending scale passages (later ascending passages) in semiquavers, each bar ending with a broken chord.

Mozart used a German folk-tune as a basis for the first-movement theme and variations of his sonata in A major K331

Mozart: Piano Sonata in A, K 331 (Air and Variations)

The variations twist and turn into many shapes but the decoration always follows the basic outline of the chords and melody heard in the original theme.

Variation 1: delicate wave-shape figures oscillating about the theme.

Variation 2: the left hand spreads out the chords (Alberti bass) in triplets with chromatic notes. The right hand embellishes these with trills.

Variation 3: changes to the tonic minor. Both hands weave around the theme and harmony in semiquaver patterns.

Variation 4: the left hand crosses the right and plays the theme shape in 3rds.

Variation 5: a slow and highly decorated version.

Variation 6: the rhythm changes to four beats a bar.

Though especially common in the Baroque Period (about 1600–1750), variation forms have been used by composers right up to the present day. You should play, listen to and study the following examples. By doing this you will discover some of the many ways in which composers create melodic and rhythmic ideas from a short repeated bass line, chord pattern or simple theme.

Byrd: *Carmans Whistle*
Purcell: Dido's Lament (from *Dido and Aeneas*)
Bach: Passacaglia in C minor for organ
     Chaconne for solo violin
     Crucifixus (from Mass in B minor)
Beethoven: 33 Variations on a Waltz by Diabelli, Op. 120
        Piano Sonata in A flat (Op.26), 1st movement
Schubert: Air and Variations in B flat
Mendelssohn: *Variations sérieuses*
Britten: Passacaglia (from *Peter Grimes*)
Hindemith: String Quartet No.4 (Finale)
(Also the blues, boogie-woogie and the big band 'riff')

To sum up:
The theme and/or chord pattern can:

1. Be decorated with embellishments.
2. Change time signature/rhythm.
3. Change tonality – major or minor.
4. Change texture – for example, thick to thin.
5. Change shape by adding other notes (wave, arch, bowl shapes etc.).
6. Variations over a bass or chord pattern are often in two-part form.

WORK ON MELODY FROM HARMONY

1. Compose a 12-bar blues for piano using this chord pattern. Write in F major and $\frac{4}{4}$ time.

Phrase 1	Chords	I	I	I	I
Phrase 2	Chords	IV	IV	I	I
Phrase 3	Chords	V	V	I	I

Add notes such as 7ths to the basic chords to make them more colourful, and use a broken chord pattern in the left hand. The melody should use a falling pattern of notes. Introduce chromatic 'blue' notes such as flattened 3rds and 7ths.

2. Compose five variations, each in a different style, based on and around this well-known tune. The tune is in three-part form, Model 2 (A1 repeated).

Mozart: Variations on 'Ah, vous dirai-je, maman', K 265

Compare your variations with the twelve that Mozart composed on this tune.

CHAPTER THIRTEEN

Borrowed chords and altered chords

You have seen that, from the medieval period onwards, composers have used chromatic notes, intervals and chords to make their music more colourful and interesting. There is a close tie between melody and harmony in the use of chromaticism. Chromatic notes in melody, such as those used in suspensions, appoggiaturas and passing notes, have resulted in new harmonies. It follows, then, that your understanding of chords must go hand in hand with your understanding of melody and part-writing.

Borrowed chords

These are chords 'borrowed' for a moment from another key to make the music more colourful.

1. The most common borrowed chords are those from a minor key used chromatically in a major key. They include I, IV, II (diminished), lowered VI, V^9 (minor), and VII^{d7}. For example, music in C major could use any of these borrowed chords from C minor.

In this extract, Brahms inserts a G minor triad into a G major passage:

Brahms: Symphony No. 2 (3rd movement)

(G major)
* = tonic minor

Two borrowed chords from C minor (IV and II) are used here, adding a darkness and warmth to the harmonies:

Verdi: *Requiem*

(C major)

IV   II
(C minor)

2. In minor keys, I is sometimes borrowed from the major. The 'tierce de Picardie' is one example.

Byrd: *The Earl of Salisbury, his Pavan*

A minor   major I
                                                            (tierce de Picardie)

3. In Romantic music, chords are borrowed from more distant keys. This example in A major suddenly plunges on to the tonic chord of C major.

Bizet: Soldiers' Chorus from *Carmen*

This is not really a modulation to C major – there is no strong cadence, and C major is not established for any length of time. Rather, it is a widening of the tonality of A major using a borrowed chromatic chord.

Altered chords

Altered chords use chromatic notes which are not found in either the major of minor versions of a given key. The two most common altered chords are (a) augmented 6ths and (b) Neapolitan 6ths. Both chords are used (a) to decorate music or (b) to modulate to distant keys (see Chapter 14).

Chords of the augmented 6th

The augmented 6th (A6) interval, from which these chords take their name, was the result of chromatic movement of parts.

A6

If a major 3rd is added, we have an augmented 6th chord.

There are three forms of augmented 6th chord, all built on the flattened submediant and figured as a first inversion of IV:

Italian	French (adds an augmented 4th)	German (adds a perfect 5th)

$$IV^{A6}_{3} \qquad IV^{A6}_{A4 \atop 3} \qquad IV^{A6}_{5 \atop 3}$$

Augmented 6th chords can also occur on lowered 2, but these are not as common as the augmented 6ths on the flattened 6th degree of the scale. *Built on flattened submediant & Aug 6th above flat.*

Italian	French	German

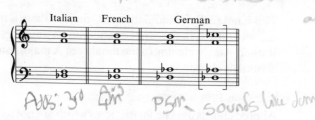

Adds: 3rd 4th   PSM sounds like dim 7th

Part-writing hints

1. Move to the A6 by step – sometimes one part may leap to one of the A6 interval notes.
2. The A6 interval, wherever it is, usually moves outwards in contrary motion by semitones.
3. A6 chords move most naturally to V.
4. To avoid parallel 5ths, the German A6 often moves to I$^6_4$ then to V. Parallel 5ths may be written when the German A6 chord moves to V, except between the soprano and bass.

Italian 6th
Play these progressions:

IV$^{A6}_{3}$　V　　　　　V^7　　　　　V　　　　　I$^6_4$　V

C major / C minor (♭)

* = appoggiatura

The Italian 6th (with its doubled 3rd) is the simplest of augmented 6th chords:

Beethoven: Symphony No. 5 (1st movement)

V^6　　　　I　　　　IV$^{A6}_{3}$　　　V

Here is an example of an Italian 6th chord on flattened 2:

Mozart: Piano Sonata in C minor, K 457 (1st movement)

C minor　　　　　　　　LII$^{A6}_{3}$

French 6th
Play these progressions:

IV$^{A6}_{A4}{}_{3}$　V　　　　V^7　　　　I$^6_4$　V　　　　V

C major / C minor (♭)

* = appoggiatura

The French 6th has the interval of a major 2nd or minor 7th and an augmented 4th as well as the A6 interval:

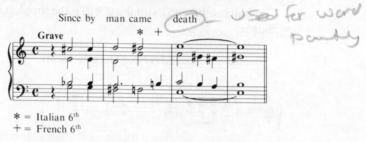

For this reason it is the most active of the A6 chords. You can compare the effect of this here – first we hear an Italian 6th; then the more dissonant and biting French 6th.

Handel: no. 46 from *Messiah*

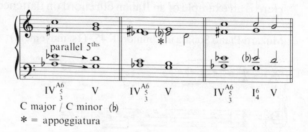

* = Italian 6th
+ = French 6th

German 6th
Play these progressions:

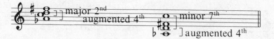

IV$^{A6}_{\frac{5}{3}}$ V   IV$^{A6}_{\frac{5}{3}}$ V   IV$^{A6}_{\frac{5}{3}}$ I$^6_4$ V

C major / C minor (♭)
* = appoggiatura

The German 6th chord is the most common of the three forms, perhaps because of its rich sound.

Gluck: 'Che farò' from *Orfeo*

(C minor)   German 6th   V

Notice the unusual voice-leading and delay in resolving this German 6th on to V⁷.

Beethoven: Six Variations on 'Nel cor più non mi sento', WoO 70

(G minor)   German 6th   V

Neapolitan 6th

Neapolitan 6th is the name given to a major chord on the flattened 2nd. It is generally used in first inversion:

LII   LII₃⁶ = LII⁶

It may be used in both major and minor keys. Like augmented 6ths, the Neapolitan 6th has a strong subdominant feel and so often moves to dominant harmony.

Part-writing hints

1. The two lowered notes usually move downwards.
2. The bass note is usually doubled.
3. The bass note moves up to 5.

Play these progressions:

LII⁶ V   LII⁶ V   LII⁶ V   LII⁶   I₄⁶ V   LII⁶ V₂⁴   LII⁶ V⁷

Play and study these examples, which illustrate some of the above resolutions of the Neapolitan 6th chord:

Sullivan: *HMS Pinafore*

1.

As some of you may know,   I prac - tis'd ba - by farming

(E minor)   I   V   I⁶   LII⁶   V   I

Beethoven: Piano Sonata in E minor, Op. 90 (1st movement)

Bach: Fugue from Organ Passacaglia and Fugue in C minor

The Neapolitan 6th is sometimes used in root position.

Chopin: Prelude in C minor, Op. 28 no. 20

During the second part of the 19th century music became more and more chromatic. Chopin, Wagner and Liszt, for example, composed highly chromatic music which tended to unsettle the feeling of a fixed key. Borrowed and altered chords, 7th and 9th chords all were used freely in colourful textures and moving lines. For this reason, chromatic music is best seen as colourful texture, passing harmony and moving lines, rather than as chords with root movements and labels. This approach to harmony is called linear progression.

In this prelude by Chopin, the harmony starts simply in E minor. But from bar 3 the harmony comes from a descending chromatic bass line. There is no point in giving each chromatic chord a label. It is much better to see the harmony as linear motion, passing boldly from I^6 at the start to V^7 at bar 13.

Chopin: Prelude in E minor, Op. 28 no. 4

WORK ON BORROWED AND ALTERED CHORDS

1. Copy out and play through these extracts. Analyse the harmony by paying special attention to the borrowed chords. Write chord symbols under the stave of your copy.

Reger: *Versöhnung*, Op. 17 no. 20

Verdi: 'Ah, forse lui' from *La traviata*

Brahms: Symphony No. 3 (2nd movement)

Bach: *St John Passion*

2. Write 8 bars of harmony (SATB) in A major. Include the following borrowed chords from A minor: I, II^7, V^9 (minor), and IV.

3. Write, play and sing A6 chords (Italian, French and German varieties) in these keys (SATB):
   Major keys: G, F, E, E flat
   Minor keys: A, D, B, B flat

4. Resolve each of the chords from exercise 3 in four different ways:
(a) to V (b) to V^7 (c) to V (with an appoggiatura) (d) to I$^6_4$–V.
Play your answers.

5. Play Italian, French and German 6th chords in root position in D minor. Then follow each with a suitable resolution chord. (The two notes which form the A6 interval expand outwards by semitone.)

6. Copy, play and analyse the chords in these extracts, which include different varieties of A6 chords. Identify the type of augmented chord used.

Beethoven: Piano Concerto No. 3 (1st movement)

Mozart: Piano Sonata in A, K 331 (Rondo alla turca)

7. Write 8 bars of harmony (SATB) in a minor key of your choice. Include all varieties of the A6 chord.

8. Write, play and sing the Neapolitan 6th chord in the following keys:
   Major keys: B flat, E, F
   Minor keys: G, F sharp, D

9. Add a suitable chord to resolve each of the Neapolitan 6ths from exercise 8. Resolve each in three different ways.

10. Copy, play and analyse the harmony (including Neapolitan 6ths) in the following extracts.

Mozart: Piano Concerto in A, K 488 (2nd movement)

Musorgsky: Varlaam's Song from *Boris Godunov*

11. Compose a flowing piece for piano (18–24 bars) which includes a variety of borrowed and altered chords.

12. Write 8 bars of harmony (SATB) in a key of your choice. Include three borrowed chords, a German 6th and a Neapolitan 6th.

13. Compose a piece for flute and piano accompaniment in three-part form. Parts 1 and 3 should use mainly diatonic chords in a suitable style. Part 2 should start with chord I in the dominant key. Progress slowly down in semitones (linear motion) to reach chord I of the home key for the start of Part 3. Use borrowed and altered chords to accompany the descending chromatic bass line of part 2.

Melodic and harmonic rhythm

Rhythm in music comes mainly from melody and/or harmony. In its widest sense rhythm is the gait, the movement, the flow of music. You can hear this in a number of ways.

1. Rhythm and melodic climax. The distance between climax notes in a number of phrases can be equal. This spacing is symmetrical as the climax note occurs regularly at the same point in each phrase.

Mozart: Symphony No. 40 (1st movement)

* = climax notes

The distance between climax notes can also be irregular, that is, asymmetrical. In this example the four climax notes are less predictable, occurring at different points in the phrases.

Bach: Air from French Suite no. 2

* = climax notes

2. Rhythm and accompaniment patterns. The accompaniment figures or patterns may

a) be the same throughout a composition:

Beethoven: theme from Six Variations WoO 70

b) become faster, giving the music a stronger, more intense flow:

Beethoven: Piano Sonata in F minor, Op. 57 (2nd movement)

c) become slower, making the music less tense or more relaxed:

Granados: *Vals poetico* no. 6

3. Rhythm and phrase lengths. Phrase lengths may be:

a) Symmetrical – equal throughout a composition. This gives the music a regular and balanced feeling of rhythm.

b) Uneven or asymmetrical. Phrases of different lengths give the music a variety and contrast.

c) A mixture of symmetrical and asymmetrical. Compare the two different effects here. Phrases 1, 2 and 3 are regular and symmetrical. Phrase 4 is irregular (asymmetrical) to provide contrast:

Mendelssohn: Violin Concerto (slow movement)

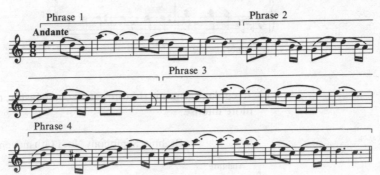

4. Harmonic rhythm. The speed at which chords change can affect the rhythm of music.

a) Regular harmonic rhythm may have chord changes

i) on each beat:

Bach: chorale from Cantata no. 78

I   I⁶ VII^{d7} I   II⁶₅ V⁷   I

ii) less often, for example, one chord a bar or one chord every two bars, as in the next example:

Beethoven: *Egmont Overture*

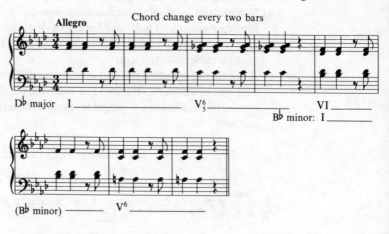

b) Irregular harmonic rhythm can become faster, making the music more intense:

Brahms: Symphony No. 1 (4th movement)

or slower, making the music more relaxed:

Beethoven: Piano Sonata in C sharp minor, Op. 27 no. 2 (1st movement)

* = chord change

Sometimes a slower harmonic rhythm combined with other energetic ingredients can make the music more exciting:

Chopin: Polonaise in A, Op. 40 no. 1

* = chord change

5. Tempo and harmonic rhythm. It is important to hear music as well as to see it. A chord, no matter how short, is *seen* as a chord. In fairly slow-changing harmonies chords are also *heard* as separate chords. But in faster-changing harmonies we tend not to hear each chord individually, only the accented chords of each bar.

To clarify this important point, *look* at this extract of piano music. You will *see* several chords in each bar:

Schumann: Finale from *Carnaval*, Op. 9

Now *listen* to the same example. The harmonies you will *hear* most clearly are these:

6. Rhythm and harmonic activity. In music of simple harmony, the introduction of a more complex or more colourful chord adds to a climax.

Beethoven: Piano Sonata in E flat, Op. 31 no. 3 (Trio)

* = climax

Several more complex chords will build up the harmonic rhythm, making it even more intense.

Grieg: Poetic Tone Picture in F, Op. 3 no. 5

Tension in harmonic rhythm can be introduced or increased by using one or more of the following:

1. Dissonant or more dissonant chords.

2. Dissonant embellishing notes.

3. Strong or stronger root movements.

4. Faster harmonic rhythm.

5. Chromatic chords or chromatic movement, especially following diatonic chords.

6. Modulation – fast and abrupt modulation is more forceful than gradual modulation.

This minuet is in three-part form. Notice how the harmonic rhythm increases in tension towards the end of Part 1 and throughout Part 2.

Mozart: Piano Sonata in E flat, K 282 (Minuet I)

Part 3 follows with parts reversed and ends in tonic key (B♭)

Different ways of using melodic and harmonic rhythm are often blended together in a complete and integrated way. Try to identify the ways in which composers use rhythm and how it affects the style of their music. Keep your eyes and, more importantly, your ears open in the music you play and listen to.

WORK ON MELODIC AND HARMONIC RHYTHM

1. Copy and play the following two melodies.

a) Identify the climax notes by marking an asterisk (*) on your copy of the music.

b) Is the melodic climax symmetrical or asymmetrical?

c) Write a sentence about the style of each melody, discussing the melodic shape and melodic climaxes.

Saint-Saëns: The Elephant from *The Carnival of Animals*

Bach: Allemande from French Suite no. 6

2. Compose two 16-bar melodies (i) for cello with symmetrical climaxes, and (ii) for clarinet with asymmetrical climaxes.

3. Compose a 4-phrase melody for violin with piano accompaniment with symmetrical phrases. The accompaniment pattern should remain the same throughout.

4. Compose a 4-phrase melody for trumpet with piano accompaniment with asymmetrical phrases. The accompaniment patterns become slower towards the end of phrase 3 and throughout phrase 4.

5. Analyse the phrase structure in this melody. Are the phrases symmetrical, asymmetrical or a mixture?

Write a piano accompaniment in which the rhythm becomes faster in phrases 3 and 4.

Brahms: Symphony No. 1 (last movement)

6. Copy and play these extracts.

Beethoven: Piano Sonata in F minor, Op. 2 no. 1

Tchaikovsky: *Chanson triste*, Op. 40 no. 2

Grieg: Scherzo-Impromptu, Op. 73 no. 2

3.

Is the harmonic rhythm regular, irregular, or a mixture of the two? Indicate the chord changes on your copy of the music.

Write a sentence or two on the way harmonic rhythm affects the style of the music. What, for example, happens to the style of the music when harmonic rhythm becomes faster or slower?

7. Compose a piece for brass quartet (two trumpets, two trombones) in two-part form (see Chapter 10). The harmonic rhythm should be regular in part 1, and irregular (becoming faster) in part 2.

8. Compose a short piece for piano where the harmonic rhythm becomes slower but the music ends with a climax. You will need to use other ingredients (for example, dynamics, rise in pitch level, chromatic notes) to achieve the climax as the harmonic rhythm slows down.

9. Tension in harmonic rhythm can be increased by introducing one or more of these ingredients:

1. Dissonant or more dissonant chords.
2. Dissonant embellishing notes.
3. Strong or stronger root movements.
4. Faster harmonic rhythm.
5. Chromatic chords or movement.
6. Modulation, especially fast or abrupt.

Play this short piece, then:
a) analyse its form
b) identify where the music becomes more intense
c) which of the six ingredients contribute to this intensity and where?

Schumann: Valse allemande from *Carnaval*, Op. 9

Modulation to remote keys

A closely related key has the same key signature as, or just one accidental different from, a given key (see Chapters 5 and 6).

A remote or distant key has a signature of two or more accidentals different from a given key. Distant modulations are often used in strongly emotional music. In the 17th century Monteverdi used remote keys to make his music both colourful and dramatic. Distant modulation became a feature in the music of Beethoven and a hallmark of later Romantic composers such as Wagner and Liszt. The distance between different keys can clearly be seen in the circle of 5ths diagram which is rather like a clock-face.

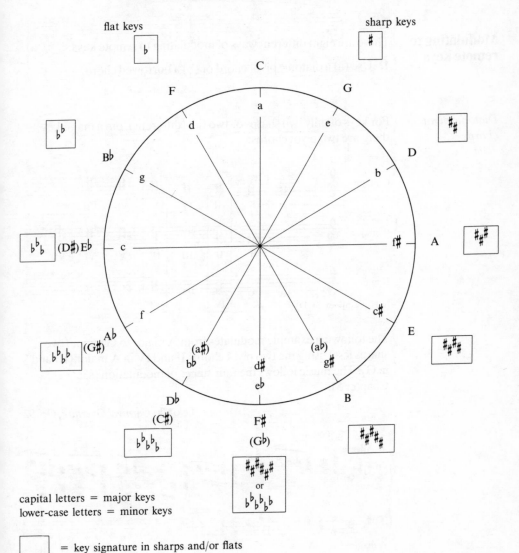

capital letters = major keys
lower-case letters = minor keys

= key signature in sharps and/or flats

Modulation to sharp keys moves round the clock-face in a clockwise direction. Modulation to flat keys moves round the clock-face in an anti-clockwise direction.

Some keys are more remote than others. For example, a modulation from G to A major (two sharps different) is not as remote as a modulation from G to B major (four sharps different). A modulation from C to B flat major (two flats different) is not as remote as a modulation from C to A flat major (four flats different). The most distant or remote modulations are those keys opposite one another on the clockface, for example, C to F sharp major, or A to E flat major.

Modulating to remote keys

There are eight different ways of modulating to remote keys.

1. Use (a) a diatonic pivot chord or (b) a borrowed chord.

Diatonic pivot chords

For keys of only two sharps or two flats different from a major key, there are two pivot chords:

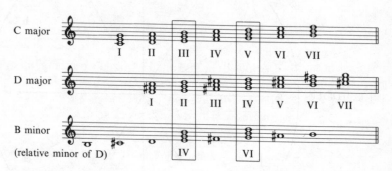

The following example modulates from A major to G major (two sharps less) using the two pivot chords II and IV in A major (III and V in G). The music follows the four stages of modulation (see Chapter 5).

Dvořák: *Carnival Overture*, Op. 92

A major: IV   II
G major: V   III   I   V   I   V   I   V   I⁶   V   I

Borrowed
chords as pivots   Distant modulations from major keys often use minor I, IV, LVI or LIII:

Chopin: Prelude in E, Op. 28 no. 9

E major: V⁷   I   V   I minor IV
             F major: III   I   V   I   IV

Borrowed chords I and IV from the tonic minor key guide the music to keys with more flats (or fewer sharps). Minor I (E minor) is used here in a modulation from E major to lowered VI (C major), with four fewer sharps.

Beethoven: Piano Sonata in C sharp minor, Op. 27 no. 2 (1st movement)

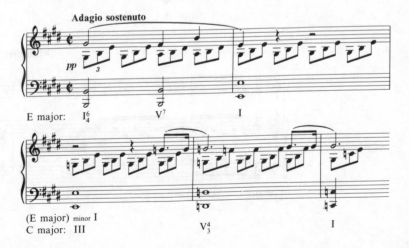

E major: I⁶₄   V⁷   I

(E major) minor I
C major: III   V⁴₃   I

Borrowed chords are not often used as pivots in distant modulations from minor keys. One obvious exception is when major I is introduced in a modulation from a minor key to its tonic major.

Schumann: *Die beiden Grenadiere*, Op. 49

* = tonic major

2. Use a single note as a pivot.

Here are some examples for you to play and study. Note 1 can link chord I in the tonic key to chord I in lowered VI key.

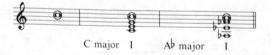

Schubert: 'Du bist die Ruh'

Note 3 links chord I in the tonic key to chord V in major VI key.

C major I   A major V   I

Gounod: *Faust*

Bb major V   I   V^7 I

G major V$^4_3$ I   IV   I

Note 3 links chord I in the tonic key to chord I in major III key.

C major I   E major I

Schubert: Waltz in A, Op. 50 no. 13

A major   I

C# major I   V^7 I

Note 1 links chord I in the tonic key to V⁷–I in lowered II key.

C major I   Db major V⁷   I

Debussy: *Doctor Gradus ad Parnassum*

C major I   IV⁶₄   I   Db major V⁷

I   IV⁶₄   I

Experiment with other possibilities at the piano. For example: note VII can link chord V in the tonic key to chord I in major 7 key.

C major V   B major I

3. Use the diminished 7th chord (VII^d7) as a pivot by changing one or more of its notes enharmonically. The changed chord then often moves to V of the new key (or sometimes I⁶₄–V).

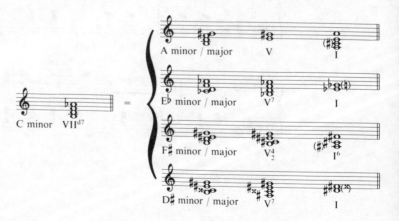

C minor VII^d7 =

A minor / major   V   I

Eb minor / major   V⁷   I

F# minor / major   V⁴₂   I⁶

D# minor / major   V⁷   I

Here is just one example of this type of modulation to a distant key. VII$_2^4$ in G minor becomes VII$_2^4$ in E minor when there is an enharmonic change from note E flat to D sharp. The change is followed by V^7 in the new key.

Beethoven: Piano Sonata in C minor, Op. 13 (1st movement)

G minor: VII$_2^4$ I^6 VII$_2^4$
                             E minor: VII$_2^4$ V^7 I$_4^6$

4. Use altered chords as pivots to distant keys. The German augmented 6th chord is the same in sound as V^7 in the key a semitone below the tonic.

Beethoven: Symphony No. 4 (1st movement)

B major   V^7

A$_3^6$ of B♭ major

B major   V^7

B♭ major A$_5^6$ I$_4^6$

The Neapolitan 6th is the same as chord I in first inversion in the key a semitone above the tonic.

C major   LII^6 C major   I^6
D♭ major   I^6 V^7 I   B minor   LII^6 V   I

Here is just one example:

Beethoven: Piano Sonata in E, Op. 14 no. 1 (3rd movement)

5. Use sequences in distant modulation, for example:
a) moving through the cycle of 5ths:

Wagner: Die Walküre

b) a repeated pattern one tone lower for keys two sharps less or two flats more each time; or a repeated pattern one tone higher for keys two sharps more or two flats less each time:

Chopin: Polonaise in A, Op. 40 no. 1

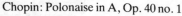

c) a repeated pattern a minor 3rd higher leads into keys three flats apart:

Wagner: Pilgrims' Chorus from *Tannhäuser*

6. Use chromatic bass movement for modulations to distant keys.

This example starts in B major. The bass falls chromatically leading to V and then I in C major – a modulation of five sharps less.

Liszt: 'O Liebe' from *Liebesträume*

Bach uses chromatic bass movement here to modulate by sequences through G major, A major, B minor and E minor:

Bach: Air from Orchestral Suite no. 3

7. Use abrupt modulation by leap. Composers sometimes leap straight into a remote key, often after a cadence or section of a piece. This example, however, leaps dramatically from E major into C major in the middle of a phrase:

Beethoven: Piano Sonata in C, Op. 2 no. 3 (2nd movement)

E major: V^7 C major: I V^6 I V^4_3 V^6 V^4_3 I V^4_3 I^6 I

Notice how these abrupt modulations are often linked by a semitone step in the melody and/or bass.

Liszt: 'O Liebe' from *Liebesträume*

Ab major   B major

◯ = semitone step

8. Side-step into a distant key. In this method of modulating, the music suddenly steps into the new key a semitone higher or lower:

Grieg: Scherzo-Impromptu, Op. 73 no. 2

A major

side steps into –

Bb major

WORK ON MODULATION TO REMOTE KEYS

1. Copy, play and analyse these extracts. In each case, say:

a) what key(s) the music modulates to

b) how remote the key is from the original key (for example, C major to A flat major is a distance of four flats, D major to E major is a distance of two sharps)

c) which of the eight methods of modulating to remote keys is used.

Schubert: Scherzo in B flat, D 593 no. 1

Elgar: Variations 8 and 9 from *'Enigma' Variations*

Bach: Fantasia from Organ Fantasia and Fugue in G minor, BWV 542

(D minor)

* = appoggiatura

Liszt: *Consolation* no. 1

Verdi: Act II Scene 2 from *Aida*

2. Remind yourself of the eight methods of modulating to remote keys. Then continue this phrase in eight different ways to illustrate each of the methods. Select your own keys for the modulations. Play your answers.

E minor or E major (♯)

3. Write four-bar phrases to illustrate modulations from:
a) E flat major to F major using a diatonic pivot chord (either III or V) (follow the four stages of modulation in this example)
b) B major to G major using minor I (B major) as a borrowed pivot chord
c) F major to D flat major using a single note as a pivot
d) G major to E major using a single note as a pivot
e) G major to B major using a single note as a pivot
f) F major to G flat major using a single note as a pivot
g) D minor to B minor using VII^{d7} enharmonically
h) G minor to B flat minor using VII^{d7} enharmonically
i) A minor to D sharp minor using VII^{d7} enharmonically
j) F minor to E minor using a German augmented 6th chord as a pivot
k) G major to A flat major using the Neapolitan 6th as a pivot chord

l) C major to C flat major using the cycle of 5ths. Start on chord I, then continue the pattern down a 5th or up a 4th until you arrive at the new key (add accidentals where appropriate)

m) G major to A major to B major using a repeated pattern one tone higher each time

n) C major to E flat major to G flat major using a repeated pattern a minor 3rd higher each time

o) B minor to E minor using a chromatic bass line

p) B major to G major by an abrupt leap into the new key

q) F sharp major to F major by side-stepping into the new key

4. Compose a piece for piano (16–24 bars). Include three modulations to remote keys using any method(s) of your choice.

The use of music and its influence on form

When composing, you may well start with some short and simple motive ideas as the basis for your composition. As you begin to shape and develop these ideas you will need to have some idea of the general style, design and form your piece will take.

You have seen repetition and contrast, unity and variety, symmetry and asymmetry, activity and rest at work in many different types of music. Forms are not so much ready-made moulds for your music, but rather general plans to help guide and unify the different parts of your composition. Forms have developed from the music written by many generations of composers. So how do composers decide which form and style to use in a particular piece? In the past, the function or use of music has often influenced its form and style.

Religious music

Religion has influenced a variety of forms in music. The singing of psalms in the early church resulted in the use of more than 3000 plain chants. These chants were a major part of Christian worship for centuries and are still used in churches today. The form of plainsong uses the natural accents of words and speech for its rhythm. Sung in unison, these free-flowing vocal lines cannot be written in time signatures with bar-lines.

Offertory for the 20th Sunday after Pentecost

The form of the chorale was also influenced by its use in church. The chorale melody was sung by the whole congregation. For this reason it was a simple tune with a slow and even pulse. Phrases were clear and regular. The melody had an even rhythm and a limited range of notes. Trained singers of the choir were able to sing more difficult music and so chorale harmonisations were rich and ornate.

Bach: chorale *Christ ist erstanden*

Dance music and form

Dance music, whether an ancient pavan or modern rumba, needs a clear pulse, strong rhythmic pattern and variety in its repeated phrases. Dance patterns have influenced music for the past 600 years. Not only did composers write music for dancing, but dance forms have been used in a great variety of other music.

In Europe, dance patterns have resulted in symmetrical phrases and forms–the repeated phrase, sentence, two- and three-part forms.

As a result of dance patterns, rhythm has become one of the most important ingredients of music from every corner of the globe. The pavans of Byrd, gavottes of Bach, Mozart's minuets, Chopin's mazurkas and Strauss's waltzes are all based on dance patterns.

Byrd: *The Earl of Salisbury, his Pavan*

Bach: Gavotte from French Suite no. 6

Mozart: Piano Sonata in E flat, K 282 (Minuet I)

Chopin: Mazurka in G minor, Op. 24 no. 1

J. Strauss: waltz *The Blue Danube*, Op. 314

The instrumental suite of the 18th century began as a collection of different dances. It became the basis for the *concerto grosso*, solo concerto, overture and even the symphony. 20th-century composers such as Stravinsky and Bartók have used dance patterns as a basis for their compositions.

Bartók: Stave Dance from *Six Romanian Folk Dances*

Dance forms from other countries such as Spain, South America, Russia and Greece have also interested 20th-century composers. The rhythms of jazz have been influenced by dance patterns. In turn, some of the ingredients of jazz have influenced important 20th-century composers such as Stravinsky (*The Soldier's Tale*, *Ebony Concerto*), Gershwin (*Rhapsody in Blue*, Concerto in F), Ravel (Sonata for violin and piano) and Copland (music for the theatre).

The composer's inner thoughts and asymmetrical form

Religious music and dance forms often served social purposes for people's activities. Composers have also been inspired by their innermost feelings. The personal, often secret world of the composer's mind has resulted in compositions of vision and free expression. This is the music which is free-flowing, asymmetrical, irregular, often slow in tempo. This very personal and inspired view of the composer can be heard in music such as free-flowing Gregorian chant, the chorale preludes and choral works of Bach, the slow movements of Beethoven's piano sonatas, the elusive harmony and shapes in the music of Debussy and Messiaen.

Beethoven: Piano Sonata in F minor, Op. 57 (2nd movement)

Debussy: 'La fille aux cheveux de lin' from *Préludes*, Book 1

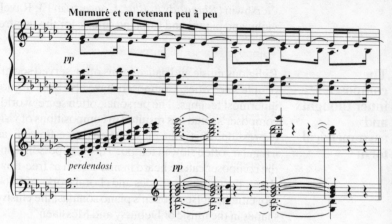

The function of music and its influence on form is best understood in short pieces – dances, songs, chorales and chants. Larger scale works often have many functions and the relationship becomes more complex and involved. The fugue for example, combines both a deep, inner expression by the composer and a high level of technical skill. At one and the same time, it is intellectual, reasoned, religious, prayerful, robust and pleasurable. Dramatic works such as opera combine function and form on a huge scale.

Within certain limits, then, especially in small-scale works, the use or function of music provides a valuable guide in our understanding and use of musical form.

WORK ON THE USE OF MUSIC AND ITS INFLUENCE ON FORM

1. Spend some time listening to and thinking about music which was composed for social purposes.

For religious music, listen to some plainsong and Bach chorale harmonisations.

For dance music, listen to the pavans of Byrd, gavottes of Bach, Mozart's minuets, Chopin's waltzes and mazurkas and Strauss's waltzes.

Think particularly about pulse, gait, rhythm and two- and three-part form.

2. Broaden your listening to include the 18th-century suite, perhaps the French suites and the four orchestral suites by Bach. Find out something about the French courante, the Spanish sarabande, the English jig and the German allemande.

3. Do some research into how dance patterns and form, together with jazz, have influenced the work of 20th-century composers such as Stravinsky, Bartók, Gershwin and Copland.

Acknowledgments

We are grateful to the following for permission to reproduce copyright material:

Edwin Ashdown Ltd for extracts from Summer and Autumn in *Seasons* by Paul Sturman © 1971 Edwin Ashdown Ltd; Boosey & Hawkes Music Publishers Ltd for extracts from *Mikrokosmos* by Bela Bartók © copyright 1940 by Hawkes & Son (London) Ltd, *Seven Sonnets of Michelangelo* by Benjamin Britten © copyright 1943 by Boosey & Co Ltd, *Billy the Kid* by Aaron Copland © copyright 1941 by Hawkes & Son (London) Ltd, *Pulcinella* by Igor Stravinsky © copyright 1925 by Edition Russe de Musique, copyright assigned 1947 to Boosey & Hawkes Inc, for all countries. Revised version © copyright 1966 by Boosey & Hawkes Inc, *Musique d'Enfants* Op. 65 by Serge Prokofiev © copyright 1936 by Edition de Musique, copyright assigned 1947 to Boosey & Hawkes Inc. for all countries; Novello & Co Ltd for an extract from *'Enigma' Variations* by Elgar; Oxford University Press for extracts from *Belshazzar's Feast* by William Walton; Universal Edition (London) Ltd for an extract from *Romanian Folk Dances* by Bela Bartók.